KNOWING WHAT YOU THINK ABOUT IS WHERE YOU WILL GO

MAKING EVERY DAY COUNT: A 7-WAY PLAN TO ACHIEVE YOUR SUCCESS

JAIRO HERNANDEZ

CONTENTS

A Free Gift to Our Readers: Download Your Master Plan For Life Journal

The Journal references a chapter-by-chapter guide with actions, steps, and strategies that follows the book to save a copy on your PC or Laptop. This will assist you in putting your Master Plan for Life in motion faster for continued success and tracking your progress so you will not have to start from scratch.

Scan QR Code to Get Access Or Visit the Link Below

https://go.f4ury.com/knowing-what-you-think-about-is-where-you-will-go

When you download your Journal, you will get a book compilation email series to assist you in staying motivated and on track throughout your journey together.

For your success!

INTRODUCTION

> *Difficulties in your life don't come to destroy you, but to help you realize your hidden potential.*
>
> — ANONYMOUS

Our life's journey is not without purpose and meaning. I came to this powerful realization at the young age of 19. In 1996, in Texas, I purchased my first book on meditation, The Silva Method, by Jose Silva. I don't believe in coincidences when everything happens for a reason, is meaningful, and is also synchronistic in everything we do in life. But something inside of me drew me to the book. I cannot fully explain it.

I just went to Barnes & Noble, and the book fell on my lap. Reading this book and absorbing its contents opened my mind to limitless possibilities for seeing the world differently. It was a life-changing encounter that led me to a better life of awareness. It also sparked a lifelong journey of learning more about the mind to understand how it works.

Then, three years later, I joined the U.S. Army, forever changing the course of my destiny. It was a life-shifting event at the time, especially given that I somehow found myself in the rough company as a teenager before joining the U.S. Army. I landed in county jail for driving under the influence of alcohol in Texas at the age of 20. The adage, "You are the company you keep," rings true as I reflect on my past.

I was born in New Mexico, USA, in 1977. My parents immigrated to the U.S. from Mexico before my siblings, and I were born, and we grew up with an abusive father and a mother who did her best to keep us afloat financially. Growing up with two siblings— an older sister and a younger brother—I was not alone in our struggles at home. We were left to our own devices and gained early independence, making decisions for ourselves. I was born mainly by nature, learning everything independently. It was tough for my siblings and me, especially with parents who spoke little English.

The environment I experienced as a child from a "broken home" was overwhelming. Making responsible decisions for my life seemed challenging until I experienced the first impactful turning point when I read *The Silva Method*. Life events always present critical junctures to experience new opportunities disguised as challenges. Both parents were too busy working on trying to make it in their new environment in the U.S., but I know they did their best for what was working for them and our family, and I am grateful for the sacrifices they had to make for us despite their struggles. However, many years passed, and I felt we were stuck in one place, not going anywhere or doing any better as a family.

After reading the Silva Method and learning more about the power of the mind and our abilities to harness it by making new choices, I was convinced that there was more to life for me. My outlook expanded as I learned about the vast opportunities we can create for ourselves when we make up our minds. I knew for the first time at the age of 19 that my thoughts and actions could keep me stuck in the same place or propel me forward in a new direction.

In 1999, when my mother decided to bail me out of jail for driving under the influence, I knew what to do. Especially when the court lowered the charges from driving under the influence to reckless driving and paying a fine, I put more effort into my thoughts and decided the best way for me was active duty in the U.S. Army. I have my older sister to thank for my decision to join the United States Army Reserves right after graduating high school in 1996. When she graduated from high school in 1995, she joined the U.S. Coast Guard, making it easier for me to find a way out of the environment I was stuck in after being arrested and going on active duty in the military. This was the best choice I could make for myself.

Qualities of persistence and determination led me to accomplish more than 20 years of honorable military service. I excelled in many areas and was promoted to higher levels of responsibility in leadership positions in no time at all. It was essential to make this severe shift in my life to live out my true potential or have a higher calling.

I was stationed in five different countries and many locations across the United States during my military career. I gained knowledge in finances, fitness, and nutrition while serving. However, the key area I have been most intrigued by for many years is how our minds work. Our environment can shape us, or we can transcend its limitations. I chose the latter.

While serving in the military, I learned so much from my leaders that I fully understood the importance of surrounding ourselves with inspiring, successful people who possess more knowledge than we do. They have the potential to illuminate our path with their wisdom. When we prepare ourselves by attaining knowledge and skills, we can serve others and be of value to our communities and the world.

I spent many hours studying meditation, reviewing books on neuroscience and other scientific studies about the power of the mind, and watching endless documentaries as part of my research. I did all of this to fully understand that there is a connection between the brain and the heart and that our thoughts and emotions impact our bodies. The brain is one of the most magnificent creations in the universe because when we learn something new, new neural pathways are created in our brains, and through repetition, we can strengthen these new learnings into powerful new habits that drive change in human behavior.

Even our memories can either hold us back in life or propel us forward if we know how to manipulate those neural pathways in our brains to work in our favor and not against us. Science tells us that everything is possible to become masters of our destiny. However, we must study it for ourselves to appreciate the wisdom behind the scientific understanding of the mind. I accept that there are some unexplainable things that science cannot clearly explain. These events remain mystical encounters–the best way I define the unexplainable.

During my days in the military, I used the information I gained through my research about the mind, neuroscience, and quantum physics to cultivate strategies to heighten awareness of equality for all. This approach also helped build leadership skills in people and enhanced team cohesion, from taking care of our bodies through daily physical activities to eating well and staying healthy. My focus was on the well-being of our service members and their families.

Getting to know the team and their families better was an essential part of the mentoring and coaching process. Finding out more about their goals was also crucial, as this was how I could further provide them with guidance, support, and mentorship. Goal setting and mentoring were critical to my team's transformation process and success. If they decided to get out, I knew I had done my best and taught them to be successful in whatever venture they chose to explore after military service.

I realized many people limit their true potential and block themselves through self-sabotage while I served in the military. When recalling my early childhood, I witnessed firsthand how things can fall apart when we succumb to merely surviving through challenges instead of stepping up and planning our days better. These words I am sharing in this book distill my life's work. We all have experienced similar life challenges and events that shape our habits, thoughts, and decision-making.

The vision for the book you are about to read or listen to can be summed up in the following words, "Our past does not define who we are, but who we will be in the future." My goal is to get you back on track with what is most valuable to you, set new goals, and stick to them. If you follow through, you will be solidly empowered to start your new authentic life journey in a few days.

I have assisted thousands of others through my military service to help them make powerful new choices for themselves. This insightful book is a further manifestation of my love for teaching. It all boils down to having a mindset of curiosity and being open to learning new things. This is how we shift our thoughts and transform our lives through our subconscious mind.

When we become aware of our thoughts and emotions and become observers of these thoughts and behaviors, we realize where we need to go in life. My philosophy is simplified as follows: "Life is a series of synchronistic encounters leading us to unknown new possibilities—when we are conscious of these blessings, good or bad." Knowing and accepting that life is a big learning lesson will help you overcome setbacks and become who you are meant to be.

In my quest to spread transformative education, I have also created a unique online community called F4URY.com. Here you will also find the necessary resources in one place to discover new ways of finding meaning in life. The focus of F4URY is on educating the community about health, love, wealth, and happiness. It is important to me to spread my teachings far and wide across the globe.

Many other vital events occurred in my past while I was growing up and serving in the military. I could have gone in any direction, choosing to quit or give up, but I always listened to my inner voice and enjoyed the journey—regardless of what direction life took me. I am not saying that everything in my life is peachy fine. Furthermore, I have had my fair share of life's knocks and undesirable situations happen, and I will possibly continue to encounter new challenges as I continue to shift my awareness.

When we have control over where we want to be because our future is determined by what we think we can achieve, our environment and past do not have to be the excuses we make for falling short of achieving success. It is more about how you think, what you do, and the steps you are willing to take to create a new inspiring reality.

Anyone can change their path or direction in life, but it is up to you to decide on the way forward. You will discover in this book so much more than the importance of goal setting and planning. This is only one part of creating a successful, achievable life. The missing piece of the puzzle is for you to understand how the mind can work for us or against us. This will be one of the most significant learning encounters for you in this book.

Once you learn more about the power of your thoughts and beliefs, you can start questioning them to change them effectively. When we better understand why we think the way we do, the goal or objective will fall into place, and we will have a better chance of achieving the desired goal at a much faster pace than we think we can.

Knowing What you Think About is Where You Will Go will unpack a powerful 7-way plan to achieve success in all areas of your life. Are you ready to change your life? Let's dive in and get started on this incredible journey together!

1

OUR BELIEF SYSTEM AND ITS EFFECT ON DECISION-MAKING

> *Man is made by his belief. As he believes, so he is.*
>
> — WOLFGANG VAN GOETHE

WHAT IS A BELIEF?

Our beliefs shape our world and experiences and impact how we see the world. When we live according to our thoughts, we put on glasses that reflect our views in every situation, event, and decision. All of this develops around the belief systems hardwired into our subconscious mind. It happens unconsciously at times, and we are unaware of why we think the way we do. At other times we are aware of it and operate from them.

Beliefs create personal truth in our perceptions and bring to life what we hold sacred in our hearts and minds. Our beliefs are the filter that determines how we interpret everything that is taking place in our lives. We give life to it further when we make decisions based on our belief system. Since childhood, we've been hearing things from others and learning what is acceptable and not from our environment, personal events, and socialized knowledge passed on from others. These reflect some of the beliefs we have adopted in our lives.

Once a belief is hardwired in our subconscious, it directs more thought processes to support it and harness its power to create an outcomes-based reality.

This is how we convert our beliefs into actionable outcomes. Some experts say that our beliefs create emotional responses to situations that do not meet the standards set by our internal beliefs. If you think about it, it makes sense. We often get irritable and emotional when something happens in our lives that fall outside the scope of our beliefs about what is right or wrong.

Beliefs, therefore, manifest in the subjective opinions we hold as true about ourselves, our capabilities, and how far we are willing to go in life concerning our goals, desires, and dreams for the future. It can determine whether we win or sell ourselves short by succumbing to negative self-talk, the internal chatter within us. For example, I followed the little inner voice that propelled me to join the U.S. Army based on the belief that I had more significant potential worthy of exploration.

I also sensed a flourishing career in this field. The little voice propelled me forward, encouraging me to avoid mediocrity. Thus, my subconscious mind accepted a new reality based on my new belief about my potential. This, in turn, pivoted me away from the rough company I was keeping at the time in my young life. My new belief about my potential moved me forward to learn new skills from leaders in my chosen profession.

Sometimes we unconsciously develop beliefs that do not benefit us. We also sadly accept these beliefs as truth. This happens when we consistently think negative thoughts about ourselves, put ourselves down, and then take this as truth. All beliefs may not necessarily be true. However, what is important to remember is that we have become socialized to accept certain beliefs about our potential as truth.

We might not even be aware of this. Beliefs include the internal positions we accept about things like the importance of our health, the acquisition of wealth, success, and the worthiness of following a particular profession. Your belief can extend to how worthy and deserving you feel about success. The limiting beliefs we may also hold to be true can be shifted, as you will learn further in this book. As we expand on our understanding of the brain and its functions with our thoughts and beliefs, we will see the light and realize how easy it is to decide on a new set of beliefs.

We will inevitably shift some of our beliefs when pushed forward by a desire to learn more and grow. When this occurs, we also change our body's biochemistry (Rao et al., 2009). We will greatly benefit from these changes when we shift our beliefs to more favorable ones. New, fresh learning outcomes can tremendously impact our perceptions and beliefs. Think of your belief as a magic wand that can transform any area of your life by simply swishing it in a new direction with an internal desire to switch to a new belief that will be more supportive of an expanded outlook on life.

As you will learn, thoughts and beliefs are integral to our brains. Changing our thoughts and beliefs to reflect what we truly desire in life will dramatically impact our brain's biochemistry and, hence, the outcomes of our efforts. This is the journey we are taking to fix areas of our lives based on our beliefs to get those areas to work better for us as we desire (Rao et al., 2009).

HOW DO WE FORM BELIEFS?

Neuroscience has proposed that unless we challenge and question our beliefs, we will be challenged by them in a manner that keeps us looking for answers only in one direction. Consider this fact: When we came into this world, we had no beliefs about anything until our brain started developing, making sense of its environment, and learning through everyday encounters. This was when we began to encode such experiences as beliefs (Haas, 2011).

Eventually, we learned things about ourselves and were told that when something happened to us, it was either good or bad. This was when we started to label our experiences accordingly to make sense of everything happening in our lives. Eventually, we developed a belief system based on these learned experiences, what our parents taught us, and our teachers, friends, colleagues, society, etc.

People tend to hold on to their beliefs pedantically, whether true or not. Limiting beliefs, for example, can be confronted head-on to avoid a stereotyped approach to life that limits your potential. For instance, if someone is exposed to much verbal abuse, they could start accepting the abuse as a reflection of the truth about who they are. This is how, in some cases, limiting beliefs are formed. When a person is consistently criticized, they can believe they will not amount to anything in life and thus adopt a limiting mindset about their potential.

No matter the circumstances, we all have a choice to think our way out of unpleasant situations. It is a deliberate choice that we can make when confronted with challenges. We must decide not to let these situations rule our minds, nor should we allow unpleasant memories to become hardwired in our brains. When we do this, we are simply setting ourselves up for self-sabotage.

Regardless of the nature of past events, they are placed in the mind through neurological connections in the brain. When a significant emotional event happens, it can keep us in a rut or propel us to experience trans-formational excellence. This is why beliefs, whether limiting or not, including our core values, must be challenged if we want to create meaningful change in our lives.

Neuroscience tells us that beliefs that are not deliberately challenged, whether they are pulling us down in life or not, will always win in our minds. This means we must develop curiosity, consistently challenge our belief systems, and be resilient to defend against limiting beliefs, whether injected externally or internally into our consciousness and minds.

As we look deeper into our belief system, it must be asked whether it is serving us and "how" it is helping us. In reality, something or someone has taught every learned behavior or belief, and it gets implanted in our brains. If we do not have other outside sources that challenge an idea or thought, those ideas will be hard-wired into our brains to be accepted as truth.

Getting out of our comfort zones, exploring new ideas, doing research, and being inquisitive about things, subjects, and other activities that interest us will significantly benefit the development of our minds, thoughts, and choices. Seek to question, explore, and encounter new things, and set yourself free from limitations. In Chapter 3, we will dive deeper into limiting thoughts and beliefs. We will also discover ways to escape these limiting thoughts and beliefs.

Our beliefs are formed by learned behaviors from family, friends, social media, the internet, TV, and politics. Therefore, we can say that all stimuli influence what we believe in. Some of these ideas can keep us trapped in socialized ideas only and NOT the truth. This is also where we must start making distinctions in our belief system; between theories and reality. When we learn something new and embrace it, a value and a belief are created in our subconscious mind. When repeatedly accepting these beliefs and values, new neural connections are made in the brain by these repeated thoughts.

The idea behind questioning our beliefs is what many enlightened individuals refer to as "becoming observers of our thoughts, decisions, and actions." Doing this empowers us to be more enlightened about how we choose to live. In this state of reflective awareness, we can also begin to harness our abilities to make new enlightened choices that better serve our goals, our state of wellness, and how we contribute to our communities and the greater world around us.

TYPES OF BELIEF

Meta: Beliefs About Beliefs

These are the core beliefs that we regard as truth. This belief system (our meta-beliefs) guides our decision-making process in everything we think and do about ourselves, others around us, and the environment. Think of your core beliefs as the glasses we wear when viewing our world, reality, and circumstances. This is how we give meaning to our experiences based on our beliefs. These beliefs also include the ideas we believe are true about other people.

The thing to remember about our belief system is that it is vast and that we mainly operate from it in a state of unconsciousness. This is because our beliefs, which govern our decision-making, feel normal. In other words, we make decisions as naturally as we breathe, based on our belief system. However, the stronger beliefs are the ones that do stand out in contrast to other views. These stronger beliefs may manifest more as habits, which can be easily deciphered as either working for us or against us (Hall, 2010).

Perceptions: Beliefs About How the World Seems, Based on Evidence

Understanding how perception works, from gathering stimuli in the environment to the mental process of digesting that information, is essential, as our belief system also guides such sensory interpretation. Beliefs are how we see the world, while perception is the conclusion we reached after examining the world through the lens of our thoughts.

Sensory information refers to how we experience sensations around us; perception is simply the interpretation of those senses. Perception can therefore be attributed mainly to our existing belief system. For example, suppose you believe that you are not good enough. In that case, you will perceive any failures you will inevitably experience through the belief that you were never good enough to begin with, and will, therefore, be unable to win in life, no matter how hard you try.

American psychologist William James said, "If we understand the world as it appears, it will be a big booming-buzzing confusion. Hence, we do not see things as they appear. Still, we see them as we want, i.e., more meaningfully" (Sharma, 2014, para. 4). According to the Principle of Perceptual Organization, William is referring to the fact that "we tend to select stimuli in situations and environments and then give them meaning."

Have you ever heard of this phrase before, "The whole is better than the sum of its parts?" This famous phrase emerged from the above phenomenon that Gestalt psychologists described. They explained the Gestalt Principle, "There is more meaning when we consider the whole picture instead of the parts that we select in forming a perception (belief) of a thing or a person" (Sharma, 2014. para. 3).

Gestalt psychologists suggest that the process of perception (forming a belief) can become more accurate when we accept that it will keep changing until we reach the whole meaning. When this occurs in the perceptual process, we obtain a fuller picture of things, people, and situations. When we reach this stage of stable perception, it is often referred to as a good gestalt (Shristi, 2017).

Suppose you consider a limiting belief when failing a task as a failure for not being good or smart enough. However, when you think about the whole situation, you might discover that it may not have had anything to do with your performance but rather other factors that came into play. If you change your belief to "I am good enough," a failure can be perceived as only a mild setback in life. You would then be willing to give it another shot while learning essential lessons from past failures (Shristi, 2017).

Opinions

They are beliefs more subjectively related to our preferences, which can result from personal biases and individual choices. Whether right or wrong, personal biases may not be based on truth or facts. Sometimes, we can develop fact-based ideas when we are prepared to gather facts to help us arrive at more objective statements. In this way, we also grow ourselves and our ability to observe our thoughts and opinions instead of being rash when forming biased opinions. Every step toward becoming more objective in our ideas will lead to more significant results in all areas of our lives.

The evidence of the value of objectivity in opinions becomes apparent when we examine our need to obtain professional ideas when it matters the most. A professional opinion is valued because it is perceived as an educated guess rather than an ill-informed one. When you are not feeling well, you tend to favor a medical doctor's professional diagnosis over that of an unqualified friend.

Predictions

These are our beliefs about how we think things will end up in the future based on what we know now. However, it is not uncommon to drum up predictions of future events based on a hardwired acceptance that history will repeat itself. These predictions are based on our human need to achieve certainty in all areas of our lives. We tend to make estimates or predictions based on the goals we would love to accomplish in each area of our lives, which all stem from our beliefs.

It is not unhealthy to visualize an outcome based on a desire to achieve a goal. It does, however, become harmful when we obsess over a desire. We do this out of fear of failure and to claim our power in every situation. Fear-based predictions are rooted in limiting beliefs, which we will explore in Chapter 3. Being mindful, present, and open to possibilities lessens our chances of making too many predictions.

We must strive to apply the magnificence of our presence "now" at this moment. This is a natural outcome of how we can effectively manifest our goals. When we make predictions based on incomplete assumptions from skewed perceptions, we anticipate repeating them in new situations, and we will self-sabotage ourselves for fear of adverse outcomes. In the next chapter, we will explore beliefs further by unpacking a neuroscientific approach to thoughts, beliefs, and their impact on our lives. However, before you proceed, let's practice some decisive, Learning-Based Action.

LEARNING-BASED ACTION

Identifying Your Core Beliefs

Let's get started and begin this first vital step toward transformation together. Remember to complete this part. Doing the work will help you better appreciate the learning outcomes, and we are preparing to achieve clarity on our way forward.

These are your action steps to achieve success in life. This will become evident throughout the contents of this book to enable you to find your full potential, waiting for you to tap into it. You will begin to rediscover yourself, empower yourself, and find your inner genius.

Step 1

Grab a pen after completing this chapter to start your "Master Plan for Life Journal." Or get access to your free downloadable *Master Plan for Life Journal*, click or copy and paste the link or go to **https://go.f4ury. com/knowing-what-you-think-about-is-where-you-will-go** save it on your PC or Laptop. This will assist you in putting your *Master Plan for Life Journal* in motion faster for your continued success when you complete each lesson in this book. We created this personal journal to help you track your progress so you will not have to start from scratch. The digital copy is designed and follows each Learning-Based Action at the end of each chapter to allow you to focus on the book's contents and your journal. In addition, you will find more tools and strategies than what is in this book, providing templated examples when you download your digital copy to help you get started on the right path to success.

Step 2

Decide to keep this journal close by for regular, insightful updates as we progress through this book together. Save it on your desktop, or keep your writing journal on hand.

Step 3

Make a list of your core beliefs in all significant areas of your life. Break it down into relevant areas like Health, Family/Relationships, Career, Finance, Education, Spirituality, Lifestyle, etc.

A current core belief in Finance could be: It is not about how much money I make; as long as I get by earning a good living, I will be okay. Do you believe the example of a core belief above empowers you to achieve financial independence or limits your prospects of earning more income? If you answer yes to the latter, this core belief makes you feel limited in choice and is undoubtedly something holding you back.

Make sure to write complete sentences that reflect your current core beliefs. Be honest, reflective, and accurate in your assessment.

Step 4

Reflect on how you feel about your core beliefs, as the above example provides.

Ask yourself: Do you feel uncomfortable? Does it feel natural and inspiring? Are you motivated by these core beliefs? Are any of these beliefs pulling you down in life?

Step 5

Identify any emotions you may feel when reflecting on these core beliefs, feel them, and describe them in words next to each identified core belief.

For example, the core belief mentioned in the area of Finance in Step 3 could make you feel as follows:

"I feel limited and unmotivated to excel in my current career because what I would love is to have a fulfilling job with greater earning potential, so while I am grateful for the work I have, I do feel stuck in a rut. Emotionally, I am feeling unfulfilled with this current core belief. It hurts me to see others prospering while I work continuously in the same job, feeling unfulfilled. I am unsure how to unhinge myself from this mindset, even though I would love more options."

Step 6

Have you identified any core beliefs that conflict with some of your goals or dreams for the future?

In this step, be honest and identify your current beliefs that conflict with your dreams of another future for yourself.

———————

Once you have identified your core beliefs, this is a critical key area in your life to break free from barriers that may be holding you back from achieving success in all areas of your life. You will now be ready to proceed to the next lesson in Chapter 2.

It is a compelling chapter in which we will take our study of beliefs to a new level of awareness by learning more about the workings of the brain. How beliefs can either support us or sabotage us from living our most inspiring life, with the neurological finding of how you can rewire the neurological connection in your brain to work for you and not against you.

2

HOW DOES A BELIEF EXIST IN THE BRAIN?

> *If you realized how powerful thoughts are, you will never think of a negative thought.*
>
> — UNKNOWN

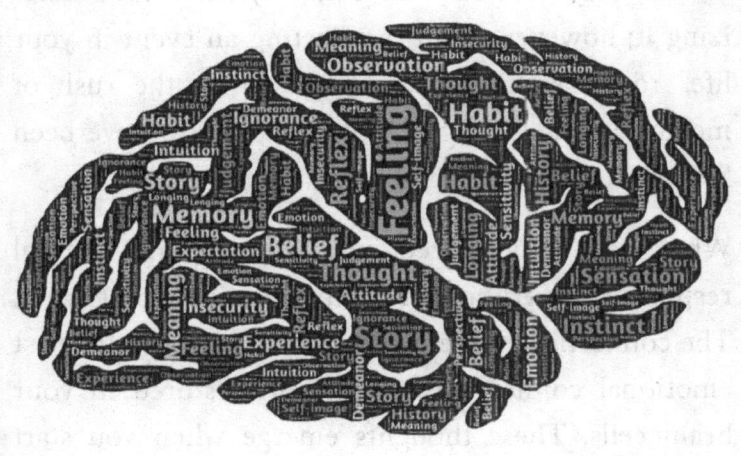

Beliefs and memories are similar when considering how they are stored inside the brain. Our memories are stored as images, thoughts, and feelings in networks made up of neurons. These are very specialized cells that make up the working units of the brain, and when stimulated by an event, the more the network is enabled by thoughts. The stronger the signal is, the more the neurons fire and the brain gets wired with beliefs, memories, and experiences coming from our thoughts.

Think of when you suffered from an emotional event in your life. The more you thought about the event, the stronger the memories emerged. Maybe you even blocked out some thoughts or memories, depending on how they affected you for many years without realizing it; however, upon recollecting an event in your life. You may have been surprised by the rush of memories that emerged, which could also have been hidden in the subconscious mind.

What you experienced was your brain's neural response to your thoughts of the emotional past event. The connections were made in the brain with the past emotional connections of memories stored in your brain cells. These thoughts emerge when you start thinking about this event, stimulating the neurons' firing and wiring.

You see, the firing of neurons strengthens the network of memories stored in your brain. This happens whenever you give a thought enough focus and energy, and the more you repeatedly think of the event, the stronger the memory. The stronger the memory, the more palpable it becomes until it almost feels as if you are reliving these memories again.

Similarly, the greater your belief in anything and the more accepting you are of its truth, the stronger the firing of neurons. According to Hebb's Law, "neurons that fire together are wired together." This means that the more you run neural networks in your brain, like memories or beliefs, the stronger they get. It is from this law in neuroscience that the wisdom of strengthening good habits emerges. Immediately, when considering this wisdom, the adage "practice makes perfect" should also come to mind (Reeves, 2018).

Therefore, achieving clarity in your views and objectives and evaluating them frequently will enhance these brain networks. According to Hebb's Law, they will anchor them firmly in the executive center of your brain, where they belong. Also, similarly when engaging in daily good, productive habits, you will be strengthening those neural pathways with a greater chance of achieving your goals. Practice makes perfect!

HOW BELIEFS CAUSE US TO BEHAVE

Since most people accept their beliefs as their truth, these internal belief systems, once wired into the subconscious mind, will give us direction and meaning in life. Remember that your beliefs are the preset filters for our perceptions. Just like a strong vision of your goal in life, the internal commands come from the executive center in your brain.

When the executive center, situated in the brain's frontal lobe, is stimulated by a vision with a map of your goal, it sets forth a clear command of action to your body and your thought processes. It will guide you forward like a captain of a ship, or a company's CEO, reminding you what you should be doing. This part of the brain has recently evolved and developed in humans, more than in any other life form.

The frontal lobe is responsible for higher functions, like planning, establishing logic, maintaining ethical behavior, setting goals, monitoring outcomes, and assessing all situations. It determines the relevance of what is most important to you and least important in your life. You can command your executive center with its vision when you deliberately choose with a significant amount of certainty and desire what it is you want and expect out of life in all essential areas (Flemming, n.d.).

Generally, you can feel disempowered, unmotivated, and somewhat "lost" when you do not have a roadmap. Think of yourself as a tourist on earth who needs to get to places A and B to explore your potential to contribute to the rest of the planet's inhabitants. Setting goals is the roadmap that will take you to your destination. Therefore, "Knowing What You Think About Is Where You Will Go" rings true when knowing how the brain operates. To achieve a clear route to your goals, stimulate the executive center and align it with your dreams' beliefs, and core values. This will get you to your destination.

When your beliefs and core values are congruent with your goals, you will have no problem setting goals. However, when they are in conflict with your goals, you will experience some resistance. This is why it is vital to continually examine your belief system and challenge those resistant thoughts. It is "you" and only "you" who can ultimately manipulate your thoughts, feelings, and actions to get to your desired destination.

You will need to look deeper within yourself to establish why there is resistance to the vision you have for your life. It would be best if you also did this before determining the most meaningful goals for you to achieve. If you do not question your beliefs, your subconscious mind, which is already hardwired with beliefs, will consistently operate from it as a truth, sometimes powerfully stopping you in your tracks.

This is one of the reasons why some people do not move forward in life. They need to change their thoughts, beliefs, and attitudes and replace them with new ones before moving forward. If I was not willing to change my thoughts and beliefs at the age of 19, when I faced a critical juncture, the chances are slim that I would've made a wiser decision for my life.

Experiencing discomfort when setting a goal can result from a limiting belief that can make you feel disempowered by a lack of purpose. Psychologists have also identified other factors influencing our decision-making and ability to set meaningful goals for ourselves. The most potent include:

Past Experience

As you already know, your previous experience will influence your decision-making. We don't need any experts to verify this for us. We, as humans, will make the same repeated choices that have worked in the past and avoid those that have not to avoid discomfort. Especially when sensing danger or fear, the amygdala, a part of the brain, activates the fight-or-flight response when there is a challenge from the unknown.

What experts do say is that future decisions that are based on past experiences may not necessarily be sound. However, when our decisions are fear-based, we will self-sabotage our efforts. This is when the brain attempts to relate a memory of the past to the present context to familiarize it with a similar situation or threat. The subconscious makes you believe there is a threat, even when there is none, unless your life is in physical danger.

For example, if you do not qualify for your dream job after applying, you'll probably tell yourself to give up on it. A limited belief is created: "You are not good enough," encoding it into your subconscious mind without noticing that you are rewiring the brain to accept this as truth. The event triggered an "amygdala" response by accepting this as a fear-based past encounter. Being aware of how past disappointing or traumatic experiences can prevent us from moving forward is essential.

Cognitive Biases

A cognitive bias is a thought-processing error in thinking. That's right! We often make mistakes in our thinking and are unaware of them. This is primarily due to our human need to always be right about things and people. It is a cognitive bias when we make rash judgments about situations and people. This occurs when our observations end up being overgeneralizations. This leads to thinking errors, which are harmful to us, and is also another way to self-sabotage ourselves by limiting our opportunities.

It often has to do with skewed memories, attention, the quality of the information available, and attribution (Cherry, 2020). Cognitive bias includes hindsight bias, omission bias, and forming stereotypes about people based on limited information. It will influence and lead to inaccurate information about others or places. For example, when considering a potential work opportunity for yourself, don't jump to conclusions about a company based only on a few observations. When deciding if the company is right for you,

you can easily dismiss the bigger picture and miss out on a lucrative business opportunity.

Keep in mind that the less information you feed your brain, the greater the chances of your thinking process being limited. Sometimes we are unaware of how cognitive biases creep into our minds. However, once these biases are given enough energy, you risk amplifying them and even turning them into beliefs. Remember Hebb's Law, "Neurons that fire together, wires together!"

The bottom line is to remember that cognitive biases will lead to distorted thinking and shortcut information processing in the brain. Not seeing the complete picture can create distress that can cause emotional imbalance, unmotivated, a limited ability to process information, and sometimes even social pressure can lead to cognitive biases (Cherry, 2020).

Escalation of Commitment

This occurs when we make risky decisions because we simply don't want to accept the fact that a venture may not be working out. A person who is heavily invested, whether financially or not, may just not want to stop believing that a venture may not be worth saving. This occurs when we spend too much time on a project and become emotionally entwined with its potential success, despite the fact that all signs indicate that success is not guaranteed to occur any time soon.

When a person feels overcommitted to a project, they are more likely not to quit in a hurry. However, there are times when we must consider the pros and cons first and do an astute assessment of the situation, investment, and real potential of the project before escalating our commitment to it.

People tend to invest deeply in projects they feel committed to, for whatever reason. Sometimes it may be a strong belief that has anchored you in a project that could end up taking more of your time and money than necessary. This is why it is essential to simultaneously assess your beliefs and priorities before escalating your commitment to a project.

Individual Differences

An apparent reason our decisions may not be accurate at times is due to individual differences. Economic factors, geographic location, age, cognitive abilities, and even physical health could influence the quality of our thought processes. Let's say age, for instance. An older person can make decisions about work that they did not anticipate in the past due to a decline in their cognitive skills. Alternatively, a more senior person may feel overconfident about their abilities, not realizing that their skills are inadequate to meet specific job criteria.

Personal relevance

Anything important to you will most likely result in solid decisions being taken to support it. Personal relevance is also significant to consider when setting up your goals. We need to ask ourselves this question: What is the point of setting goals or deciding to do something if it is not personally relevant to us? Sadly, many people do set unrealistic goals that are genuinely not achievable–not for the sake of impossibility, but more because the goals are not aligned with what is important to them, i.e., what their hearts are called to do.

You will be more than likely to achieve the goals that have personal relevance to you. When searching for meaning and purpose, we must look within ourselves to determine that purpose. Most people feel frustrated about not achieving their goals when they set unrealistic ones or ones that are based on what other people think they ought to be. With this perceived notion, it's best acceptable to seek what matters the most to you.

Like pursuing a professional singing career where you recognize you do indeed have talent. Instead, fear of failure, rejection, or success will set in, leading to a different route. We tend to place ourselves in a safer environment and work in an industry that is not genuinely nurturing our true potential because it is the norm to be safe. Rather than just taking a chance, no matter how small your talents may be, they are lying dormant inside, screaming to come out of you.

LEARNING-BASED ACTION

Dealing With the Past Head-On

We all need to deal with our pasts and reach a point in our transformation where it no longer bothers us to make fearful choices. When we understand how beliefs are implanted in the brain to cause us to behave in certain ways, we indeed have control over what we think and can decide what serves us. Fundamental transformation happens when we are willing to admit how stuck we are and do whatever it takes to get unstuck!

Now it's time to put what you learned to work and rewire your brain. By taking the steps to undo the constant harm, we are doing to ourselves by still living in the past.

Step 1

Grab your pen and journal, or open your Master Plan for Life document on your PC or Laptop and go to Chapter 2. If you have not downloaded your digital copy, click or copy and paste the link or go to **https:// go.f4ury.com/knowing-what-you-think-about-is-where-you-will-go** to get the strategies you need to implement to start believing in yourself.

Make a list of past experiences that continue to sabotage your efforts in the present moment.

Ask yourself: Are there recurrences regarding certain aspects that constantly repeat themselves in your life? Ask yourself why they continue to occur.

Be honest, have a conversation with yourself, and write it down in complete sentences.

For example, "I have tried to study several times and signed up for various courses, but I have never completed any of them. Why... It is also based on a fear of success, as I could never imagine myself succeeding. This mindset keeps me stuck, earning less money and not exploring my full potential."

Step 2

Now that you have taken note of these aspects of repeated limited thinking and disappointments–go deeper and get to the root of the problem.

Ask yourself: What is holding you back that keeps you stuck, preventing you from making new choices for yourself that will lead to new outcomes?

Step 3

Remember to consider that you may be attracting the same lessons back because your subconscious mind is already conditioned to seek out similar circumstances to be safe. That leads to the emotion of fear-based belief in scarcity, lack, failure, and success.

This is how you work out the past to accept what is not working and what is working to adopt a new, improved belief system injected into your subconscious mind.

After you have identified all the stuck areas in your life and traced them back to your past, you are now ready to move on to the next stage—rewriting your beliefs, which you will encounter in Chapter 3. You will identify any hidden fears that may still be holding you back and how to break free from limitations to be inspired to become limitless.

3

TRANSFORMING LIMITING BELIEFS INTO UNLIMITED POTENTIALITIES

Man often becomes what he believes himself to be.

— MAHATMA GANDHI

ACCEPTING THAT NOTHING IS IMPOSSIBLE

Now you know how a belief system is created in the mind and how it can sometimes disempower your efforts to succeed in certain areas of your life. We can achieve greatness in wealth, health, and happiness when we believe in it and feel deserving of it. We will dive deeper into the subconscious mind to focus on how negative thoughts and mind-chatter can lead to adverse outcomes that hold you back from achieving success. Regardless of your circumstances right now, you do have the power to change anything in your life. You better believe it because it is all about what you think.

Louise Hay lived from 1926 to 2017 and was a world-renowned expert on human behavior. Like other experts who managed to transform their own lives, she too relied on her capacity to create change from within and taught others—millions of people around the world—how to do the same for themselves. Louise linked thoughts to physical health.

She proposed that those negative thoughts, left unchecked, created disease in our bodies, and she went on to prove this in many wondrous ways. Today, there isn't a single human behavior expert or neuroscientist who will tell you otherwise. We must become conscious of the quality of thoughts we entertain about ourselves. In the words of Louise Hay, as mentioned in Sega Antonio's YouTube video (2016):

> We can refuse to think certain thoughts. Look how often you have refused to think a positive thought about yourself. Well, you can also refuse to think a negative thought about yourself. It seems to me that every person I know on this planet is suffering from self-hatred and guilt to one degree or another. The more self-hatred and guilt we have, the less our life works. We find that we cannot speak up for ourselves, and we are always trying to please others. Or we may be angry and self-explosive all the time. The less self-hatred we have, the better our life works on all levels. This includes the health of the body too.

Negativity poisons a person's mind and body. It harms our inner being because the essence of who we are, from a spiritual perspective, is perfection, far exceeding our understanding of our existence when we accept our true potentiality. Begin to tune away the negative self-talk learned from experiences or by taking on other people's limited knowledge of our true potential. Allow yourself to live a life of wonder, joy, creativity, and self-fulfilling prophecies aligned with the worth of your existence.

Lying dormant within you are the unique, inherent gifts you were born with to get curious about your existential purpose. When tapping into your unlimited potential already implanted in your mind from birth toward adulthood, you may ask, "How do I know this?" I know this from gaining insight from working with thousands of people from all walks of life while serving in the military, just like you and me. It's a common challenge we all face, living in communities bombarded with thoughts, ideas, and negatively socialized concepts that have groomed millions of people across the globe.

However, thankfully, science has also contributed to and changed this for us. Since the enlightenment began, humanity has started shifting and challenging stoic ideas and monolithic ideologies of life from the past. Ideologies are simply that—ideologies. You can create your own set of ideologies; take some from the past and from those who inspire you, then create your own based on your continuous transformation and evolution.

We achieve this when we are curious about everything that interests us and decide to expand that curiosity by chasing knowledge. When standing on the shoulders of giants that came before you, who call you with their wisdom, stand on your own two feet when you are ready to be a giant of possibilities.

THE MIND-BODY CONNECTION

Dr. Joe Dispenza is a neuroscientist who has dedicated his life to creating mindful solutions for our daily lives. According to him, we have around 70,000 thoughts daily and are unaware of about 90% of these thoughts. Additionally, approximately 70% of our thoughts are harmful; by age 35, we are so hardwired in the brain that this is how we behave in everyday situations (Dispenza, 2015).

It means that our behaviors have become automatic, with habitual responses related to our mindset and thoughts. Obvious reasons should come to mind. Unless you reflect on the consequences of your thoughts and examine your negative and limiting beliefs, you will remain stuck in this never-ending cycle of negativity, resulting in physical symptoms.

Here's how: Negative thoughts will cause you some stress, undoubtedly. This causes us to experience anxiety, fear, and sleepless nights. When bombarded with stress, our nervous system goes into flight or fight mode. Adrenalin will get the heart pumping extra hard. As mentioned before, the amygdala response is activated, and we chemically produce these stress hormones (cortisol) from thought alone. Even though stress hormones have positive benefits, the effects become damaging when they are overused.

Cortisol, when overstimulated during stressful situations, can lead to digestive issues, weight fluctuations, an increase in wrinkles, dull skin, decreased immunity, and loss of sleep. Meanwhile, some side effects of adrenalin include breathing problems, fast heart rates, nausea, vomiting, dizziness, high feelings of anxiety, nervousness, and tremors.

Short-term stress has a beneficial effect that will cause us to achieve high levels of productivity when we are determined to win and go all out to turn that desire into reality. Winning can mean different things for all of us. In this context, I am referring to the desire to win in order to reach your goals. However, long-term stress is not helpful when we label our limiting beliefs about ourselves and our capabilities. Why it is essential: Addressing how we think and feel about ourselves is a great way to shift our awareness away from negativity.

It allows us to create a new way of living when we introduce relaxation techniques, such as meditation and other self-care rituals, that boost the dopamine hormone, which is secreted from the brain. When this hormone is released, we get a rush of feeling great, especially when in tune with our dreams and desires, which will make us feel happy, alert, focused, and on fire.

It takes 66 days to develop a new habit that gives us the ability to reprogram our brains with new thoughts, ideas, and belief systems. Science tells us that our brain is neuroplastic. This means the brain has the ability to change or adapt to new learning, experiences, and memory formation throughout our life. This is why most experts encourage people to stick to a plan to form a new habit for 66 days straight. This will enable the brain to adjust accordingly, bringing about lasting change (Clear, 2018).

UNDERSTANDING THE POWER OF LIMITING BELIEFS OVER YOUR LIFE

Limiting beliefs are thoughts. They are opinions you choose to follow by repeating them daily due to some past occurrence or fear-based beliefs. Limiting beliefs are not absolute truths. They tend to harm one's life by stopping people from moving forward and growing personally and professionally.

A negative thought is a limiting belief you may have about yourself, your abilities, and your potential. It occurs when you persistently put yourself down and refuse to accept that you are truly worthy of living your best life. When we have convinced ourselves that we are unworthy of our goals, success, love, and achieving our fullest potential, those thoughts become programmed into our subconscious mind as limiting beliefs.

In the previous two chapters, I briefly introduced you to what happens when we have beliefs ingrained in the subconscious mind. These limiting beliefs hold us back from achieving our most significant potential. We are responsible for putting those beliefs into our minds by accepting them as truth. Or, we may have unconsciously accepted the opinions of others, not all of whom are qualified to determine our true potential.

Concentrate on these words: "No matter what happened in the past or is happening right 'now' or in the future. It is up to 'you' to decide how it should impact your life. Within your mind lies the greatest potential of humankind, that you indeed have unique talents and gifts worthy of exploration." Despite these intense emotions, you may be experiencing now, or from events in your past, you have the internal power to shift that energy right now.

Shifting the hardwired negative thoughts, feelings, and actions may take time. However, making decisive changes in your thoughts today towards conquering, transcending, and eliminating them from your life will set a new course of motion in your subconscious mind.

Keep practicing for the next 66 days and throughout your life to continually rewire your subconscious mind to positive ways of thinking. You will discover that you no longer think negatively. You are bound to experience a shift after making a consistent effort. Being aware of your thoughts will improve your overall health, putting the power back in your hands over which thoughts you entertain. Simply by shifting them to become more positive and enlightening, you will experience an improvement in the quality of your life.

There are numerous inspiring stories about how people have experienced massive breakthroughs after confronting the truth about their existence. Dr. John Demartini is one such person. Another exciting story is that of Hollywood star Halle Berry, who refused to entertain negative thoughts about her career prospects. She refused to give up on her dreams and wired her brain accordingly, not to accept defeat but to do whatever was necessary to continue doing what she loved and realize her greatest potential lay inside her mind.

From a High School Drop-Out to a Genius

The world-renowned "human behavior" expert Dr. John Demartini wasn't always considered a genius. He was once a high school dropout with little hope of amounting to anything. His teachers consistently reminded him of this. From an early age, he showed determination and wanted to overcome his physical disabilities. He couldn't read or write at the age of 14 and appeared to have prolonged learning disabilities. He was brilliant in sports later in his teenage years, but was born with arm and leg deformities and wore braces to straighten them out.

He enjoyed surfing at the time and felt some hope for a future in surfing. What is astonishing is that at 14, his parents dropped him off on the highway in Houston, Texas, and wished him well. Somehow, they thought fulfilling his dream of being a great surfer was worthy at the time. There he was, at 14, on his own, peddling in the streets to make a living. He slept on park benches, in 24-hour restaurants, and at the local bowling alley. He found a part-time job, and at 17, his dream of becoming a surfer was to go to Hawaii.

It was 1976, and John's life was about to change forever, even though he was homeless once again. At the time, he didn't know that his teachers and family had placed negative limiting beliefs in his subconscious mind. By accepting this "fate," handed down, John took what everyone was telling him—that he wouldn't amount to anything—as his actual reality in life, and had no chance of ever being anything more than a surfer.

In Hawaii, John had a near-death experience while surfing one day. He ate a whole bunch of poisonous plants, which is how he survived. The strychnine cyanide poisoning caused by the plant caused his muscles to spasm out, locking his fingers and toes. Stunningly, he made it to his tent from the waves, where he lay until a passing woman finally rescued him. She cleaned him up and took him to a health food store to nourish his body. There he saw a flier about a talk and a yoga session hosted by Paul Bragg, the founder of the first health food stores in the U.S.

John decided to attend. It was, without a doubt, a defining, life-shifting encounter for him. During the talk and yoga session, the 93-year-old Paul Bragg awakened in John an appetite for knowledge and told him that he could achieve anything. He also told him to repeat daily, "I am a genius, and I apply my wisdom." John's words often leave him teary-eyed, "No one ever spoke to me like that before."

From this point, he decided to change his life and take on a much larger vision than a surfer. He committed to dedicating his life to learning to read and getting an education. He also envisioned traveling worldwide and speaking to millions of people, teaching them how to maximize their human potential. He has achieved all of this, and today he is regarded as a genius. Dr. John Demartini is also among the one percent of the global population who are truly financially independent (Demartini, n.d.).

The lesson from John's story is that it just takes one powerful encounter to show you the way out. Such as this book you are reading or listening to, which has crossed your path for you to replace the limiting belief, as John did with that one fateful evening. John has written more than 40 books and has read more than 30,000 books. Just as John experienced a new awareness about his potential, so can you. It is a question of breaking free from your limiting beliefs and taking on a more inspiring vision for your life, followed by consistent action to reach your goals.

From Living in a Shelter to Becoming a Hollywood Star

Halle Berry is one of many Hollywood stars who started from humble beginnings. When she moved to New York City to become an actress, she was often broke. She ultimately found herself without cash and had to sleep in a homeless shelter. However, Halle was prepared to do whatever it took to realize her fullest potential as an actress by winning some top roles and an Oscar in 2002.

Halle worked as a waitress and a bartender and admitted that sleeping in a homeless shelter was worth it. Halle first reached out to her mother for cash but was refused, leaving her with no option but to find a homeless shelter to stay off the streets. She says that her struggles during her early acting career made her stronger. In an interview with People Magazine, Berry said, "It taught me how to take care of myself and that I could live through any situation, even if it meant going to a shelter for a small stint" (McDowell, 2019, para. 2).

Her belief system was entrenched in her longing for success and shaped her behavior accordingly, to withstand hardship even if it meant being homeless. She decided what would control her—it was not poverty but a real chance at making a great success of her career as an actress. Similarly, you decide what will control you, and your sacrifices for success are the price of the hard work you are willing to do to make things happen.

That price is focus, dedication, and absolute commitment. Deciding to do something is only the first step. Changing from within is the most significant step to take to prepare yourself for the committed action that will need to follow your intention to succeed. This is why it is important to love what you do.

UNDERSTANDING THE POWER OF THE SUBCONSCIOUS MIND

The subconscious mind is a powerful internal force that drives human behavior. It regulates the functioning of our body, and our actions are shaped by our powerful thoughts. Conscious means awareness, while subconscious indicates what is beyond our understanding. This means we are not always aware of the thoughts, feelings, and emotions that drive us because they are stored in our subconscious mind and put us on autopilot.

Your subconscious mind is responsible for all your successes and failures. For the following reason, we carry beliefs about what is possible and impossible in our subconscious mind. Your conscious mind is what you are mainly aware of, while the subconscious mind, on the other hand, works in the background. When your conscious mind wants something, it uses willpower to get it. However, if your will is weak and your desires are unreachable, it is mainly because your subconscious mind is working against them.

The subconscious mind works with the limiting belief about yourself and your desires, unless you change it to a powerful one of success. Remember, your subconscious mind is in place to protect you and is working against you, not for you. Our subconscious mind is your memory storehouse. It is where all your memories exist, whether you remember them or not. Every emotion you feel, and experience is stored in your subconscious mind.

The subconscious mind naturally guides your bodily functions, which are part of the nervous system, including breathing, blood flow, digestive processes, and all operations of your organs. Also, your emotions are subconscious, reminding you of things from your past, which will automatically protect you emotionally and physically.

Especially if you feel threatened due to negative thoughts or emotions based on similar encounters from the past or if you are facing a fierce animal, your subconscious mind will guide the nervous system into fight or flight mode. As discussed earlier in this chapter, your amygdala response is activated. Stress hormones will be released into your bloodstream to move you into action. Similarly, your subconscious mind will do the same with your beliefs to protect you from danger. It does this when your thoughts are based on fear of the unknown.

Subconscious beliefs are formed from experiences from negative and positive thoughts and events. You can instantly shift your thoughts from positive to negative. You can command your subconscious mind into a new venture by believing in yourself more and eliminating adverse outcomes. You can reprogram your subconscious by consciously removing unwanted fears and limiting thoughts. However, this is how to raise these limiting beliefs in your conscious mind: You can release them and replace them with more empowering ones (SoulStarter, n.d.).

Four Common Limiting Beliefs

There are four common limiting beliefs that most people accept as true. Once accepted as truth, these beliefs will hold us back from achieving success in all areas of our lives, whether we are consciously aware of them or not. The opportunity is for you to examine where in your life or how you have been manifesting limiting beliefs. Take a closer look at each of them to see if they have impacted your life, are keeping you stuck, and how you can overcome them.

Fear of not being good enough. Usually, this fear is based on negative thoughts. Or if someone repeatedly makes you feel inadequate by deliberately undermining you, you may conclude, naively and painfully, that you are not good enough. This is a defeatist attitude.

Not being smart enough. This limited belief will hold you back from confidently doing your best professionally and personally. You may struggle to be competitive in work situations. Additionally, I am becoming more introverted and afraid of engaging with like-minded people. You have programmed your subconscious mind to accept this limiting belief that you appear as though you are not smart enough. Therefore, you are manifesting this limited belief all the time, consciously or subconsciously, limiting your chances of rising to your true genius.

Not having enough. This limiting belief reflects a mindset of scarcity, not abundance. It is a common limiting belief among people who have started with very few possessions and opportunities in life. Maybe you were born into a family that was not generously economically endowed. Therefore you always felt condemned to living a life of scarcity as opposed to embracing a life of abundance.

Fear of success or failure. Success is a state of being who you are authentic. If you fear failure and success, you also fear being yourself completely. Failure is part of the journey to achieving success. Instead of worrying about the journey, embrace it as the best possible adventure you can have, whether you fail along the way a couple of times or not. The worst possible failure you can experience is not even trying.

LEARNING-BASED ACTION

Different Beliefs Lead to Another Life: How to Change Your Belief System Into a Positive One?

As we've already demonstrated with two case studies, you will not likely achieve great success unless you embrace a positive, more engaging belief system that supports your goals, aspirations, and life's vision.

This section will help you how to switch from a limiting belief to a more uplifting, positive one. Following this exercise will shift your mindset in seven simple steps. Go ahead and begin your journey toward making positive changes in your life.

Step 1

Grab your pen and journal, or open your Master Plan for Life document on your PC or Laptop and go to Chapter 3. If you have not downloaded your digital copy, click or copy and paste the link or go to **https://go.f4ury.com/knowing-what-you-think-about-is-where-you-will-go** to remove limiting beliefs from your life and start trusting your capabilities.

Choose the area of your life that you want to change. You should instinctively know when things are not working out for you.

If you are experiencing trouble doing this, identify where you feel uncomfortable and why.

Ask yourself: Is it in your relationships or job? Are you having difficulty studying a course, or are you afraid of making changes in any areas of your life?

Step 2

Examine all the beliefs in that area that you've already identified. Maybe you would love to make changes in all areas of your life, and why not?

Improvement is an ongoing journey, especially when aspiring to live your best life. So, go for it! Read your beliefs, and go deeply into them to assess how they are currently manifesting in your life.

Step 3

Now decide with absolute clarity what core beliefs you will change about your life and go for it!

Start rewording your core belief from "limiting" to "unlimited."

For example, if you believe that you are deserving of not having enough, change your belief to living a life of abundance.

Remember: "There is no lack in my life, I create abundance, and there is abundance available to me right now to embrace in everything I do and have!"

Step 4

Now that you have changed your core beliefs from scarcity to abundance, feeling more than good enough to achieve all your goals in each area of your life, remind yourself why you must change this belief.

Step 5

Imagine how your life can be by adopting a more unlimited mindset daily; picture your life in vivid detail in all areas; start to feel the change already on the way!

Step 6

Be mindful, reflective, and appreciative; all of that comes from your shift in beliefs and mindset.

It would be best to do this consistently when adopting a new belief system. Do this every day. Read your new beliefs and visualize your life-changing in a new direction.

As you wake up, and before you go to sleep, repeat your new belief as often as possible during the day.

Step 7

Every day, write down one to three things you will do to change your actions to reflect your new beliefs at the end of the day.

And the next day, do what you said you would do.

———————

Once you have clearly identified how to empower yourself with a new belief system, that will assist in removing limiting beliefs from your subconscious. These are barriers that no longer support us in our life journey so that we are capable of accomplishing more than we think we can.

You are now ready to move on to the next chapter to learn how we process information during everyday encounters and our environments to become more aware of identifying the needed skills we need to succeed in life.

4

UNDERSTANDING HOW WE THINK

> *Every thought that we think, is creating our future.*
>
> — LOUISE HAYE

HOW WE PROCESS INFORMATION IN OUR THINKING MINDS

Our chances of success are shaped not only by our beliefs, thoughts, and actions, but also by the skills we acquire in the learning process. In addition, belief systems directly correlate to the cognitive and metacognitive skills we receive in the learning process. This, in turn, also impacts the decision-making process and our chances of ultimately achieving success every day toward realizing our goals.

We have been engaging in cognitive learning since the day we were born. It is the process of learning new things by using our senses. Cognitive learning is not just the process involved when learning from textbooks. It also includes everyday learning experiences and acquiring new skills through experimentation and practice. Cognitive learning is a unifying process of digesting information picked up by our senses, responding to it, and quantifying that information in our minds (Lynch, 2018).

Think of a strawberry. It will be a fascinating cognitive encounter if you've never tasted one or even seen one. You would first be curious about what a strawberry is. When you learn it is a delicious, safe fruit, you will still have no complete experience beyond knowing what it is. The cognitive learning process would be complete once you taste it, allowing your senses to experience all the sensations you encounter when eating the fruit.

Your thinking mind will further assess the sensations you experienced when eating the strawberry, thus unifying that encounter with the information you received about the fruit before eating it. You might also think about your thoughts of the strawberry further to notice what first came up for you from the moment you took a bite.

The example of the strawberry is similar; we are engaging in cognitive learning when we observe our thoughts through the sensations of acquiring new knowledge. Metacognition involves thinking about our level of thinking and improving our comprehension of a situation. When we reflect on our thoughts and actions and observe the actual sensations of a learning experience, that is how cognitive learning is experienced in our environments.

HOW COGNITIVE LEARNING BENEFITS YOUR BRAIN AND GROWS KNOWLEDGE

Nothing is more satisfying to a curious mind than figuring things out about its environment and discovering new things. Once our cognitive journey begins, our search for meaning in life can lead us to make discoveries about ourselves and our world. This is how we make sense of our cognitive encounters and link them to who we are and what interests us.

We become purposeful when we develop new ideas based on our cognitive and metacognitive encounters. This thinking process can also give us direction when considering the professional career we wish to pursue. For many people, it is the beginning of their life's work and contribution. My journey began with an inspired idea to shift my life from being reckless as a teenager with poor company to having the desire to develop my potential.

My curiosity about my potential and the inner drive to succeed in life led me to join the U.S. Army. Within that journey, my interest in studying health, nutrition, fitness, finances, and how the mind works also profoundly engaged me. With this profound knowledge, I utilized this information to further develop the teams I led in the military to benefit their personal and professional development. After I retired from the military, I focused on learning digital skills, which was the next step I took to become an online entrepreneur to provide products and services so that people all over the world can get transformative education and information in one place.

This is how we grow and develop ourselves into contributing, enterprising leaders—by exploring our cognitive learning skills through educational encounters that inspire us. Inspiration is the seed of motivation planted to blossom. It is the weeds of limiting beliefs that sabotage and destroy our inspired actions. We can consistently pursue learning and growth in the direction of our most significant interests and inspirations.

Creating cognitive learning strategies should be a consistent part of our goals. We deepen our knowledge to develop sophisticated ways of solving problems around the world. Our critical thinking skills will naturally expand in the process. As we progress, we become leaders in our own right, able to see things that others may not see due to the ongoing cognitive and metacognitive learning skills we acquire in continuous learning.

Once we pursue cognitive learning experiences in the desired field of interest, we also begin creating new neural connections within our brains. When expanding our knowledge continues, it also changes and transforms our thinking minds and who we are as people of the world. This, in turn, will also impact our belief systems to be modified. Then we maximize our brain's potential when we continuously learn new information, explore existing ideas within our minds, and deepen the brain's capacity to store further information in its subconscious memory bank.

With cognitive and metacognitive learning experiences, we open ourselves up to new possibilities. When we pursue the things we love the most and open our minds to learning more about those subjects, we permit ourselves to become influential contributors. We will undoubtedly achieve personal satisfaction in pursuing knowledge.

Ways to Develop and Improve Our Cognitive Skills

Improving our cognitive skills also takes care of our physical and mental health. Managing your time effectively and exercising your brain.

Reduce stress

When we engage in conscious efforts to reduce stress in our daily lives by doing activities that improve how we feel about ourselves and our lives, we are more than likely to improve our cognitive learning skills. Spending time in nature, walking, exercising, or doing activities like yoga, meditation, and quiet relaxation exercises will improve how you deal with stress on a daily basis, leaving you feeling healthy in your body, mind, and spirit.

Take Care of Your Body

You can achieve this by fueling it with proper nutrition and care. Make healthy dietary choices, drink plenty of water, and get enough sleep to restore yourself mentally, physically, and psychologically. Sleep helps your brain sort through memories and improves your thinking abilities.

Focus Your Attention

Keep your mind alert and focused on what truly matters to you. During the day, place your attention on your high-priority activities and avoid low-priority distractions. When you have deadlines and targets, the best way to do this is to stick to the time frames by managing your time and attention. This will dramatically improve your cognitive skills.

Exercise Your Brain

When you exercise specific areas of your brain by learning, you will improve your cognitive skills. Here are some activities you can implement more frequently in your day to significantly enhance your mental skills.

- Read a book when you're ready to take a break in the day or at night before sleeping.
- Engage in brain activities like solving puzzles or mysteries.
- Play games like chess to engage your mind.
- Sing, write a story, or engage in creative art activities.

Ways to Develop and Improve Our Metacognitive Skills

Developing your metacognitive skills will help you in numerous ways to better yourself. Meditation, visualization techniques, goal setting, and asking yourself powerful questions to introspect and transform your behavior are all powerful ways to improve your metacognitive skills.

Meditation and Visualization

The most significant benefit of metacognitive skills is the ability to self-regulate your learning outcomes and create effective strategies to help you achieve your goals effectively. This is why many human behavior experts encourage meditation and visualization when setting goals. It allows individuals to get to the heart and soul of who they are and why they wish to pursue specific goals.

Take a Time-Out for Yourself

Being reflective, seeking quiet time in nature, or simply giving yourself time to enjoy hobbies that improve your state of well-being will also improve self-reflective awareness and metacognitive thinking.

Goal Setting Strategies and Monitoring Activities

Achieving clarity of purpose is the first step of embarking on a broader transformative metacognitive exercise. An enriching goal-setting process we are setting out for you here in this book is a powerful way to leverage change in your life!

Asking Powerful Questions

There is a purpose when you complete the Learning-Based Actions at the end of each chapter in this book.

First, you are rewiring the neural connections in the brain to improve new thinking processes. Second, train your subconscious to work for you, not against you. Lastly, improving your metacognitive skills— thinking about what you think about, something you can do quietly in your own time and space.

Every exercise in this book aims to help you observe your thoughts, improve your thinking and learning process, and increase your awareness of the importance of self-development and personal transformation. When we begin by asking ourselves powerful questions and answering these questions honestly, we strengthen our metacognitive skills.

Creating Strategies and Monitoring Progress

When we set goals, create strategies to reach those goals, and continuously monitor our progress and learning outcomes, we also improve our metacognitive skills. This process also helps us make necessary adjustments to our goals and strategies as we progress (Innerdrive, n.d.).

LEARNING-BASED ACTION

In this exercise, you will identify how to improve your cognitive and metacognitive skills to start changing your trajectory for your new life journey. Here you will identify the skills you need to acquire in each area of your life and be one step closer to reaching your goals.

Step 1

Grab your pen and journal, or open your Master Plan for Life document on your PC or Laptop and go to Chapter 4. If you have not downloaded your digital copy, click or copy and paste the link or go to **https://go.f4ury.com/knowing-what-you-think-about-is-where-you-will-go** to get the added reinforcements you need to set yourself up for success.

Step 2

Go to chapter 3, step 3, where you've listed the core beliefs in each area of your life and converted your limiting belief into an unlimited one.

Step 3

Identify the gaps in each area of your life by asking powerful questions to raise your cognitive and metacognitive learning outcomes.

For example: In Finance, if your goal is to earn more income, or attract additional income streams, create a strategy that is linked to your career or what you love doing, even as a hobby, and that can raise an income stream for you.

Also, identify skills you would need to adapt to move you into a higher income bracket.

Step 4

If you are struggling with any issues in each area, create a strategy to improve your relationships based on your desired outcome. Do this for all areas of your life. Reflect and ask yourself powerful questions to create an intended transformation in all areas of your life.

Step 5

Create a list of all skills needed in each area and a plan of action with a deadline for each task.

Step 6

Reflect on each area of your life, read your core beliefs, and consider all the actions you've committed to date.

Once you have asked yourself power questions to raise your level of awareness, you are ready to move on to the next inspiring chapter to learn how to identify the things you value the most. This is a crucial area that enables you to get crystal clear about what will make you the happiest and love to accomplish in the future.

5

IDENTIFYING THE THINGS YOU VALUE MOST

> *If you really want to fly, harness your power to your passion.*
>
> — OPRAH WINFREY

WHAT DO YOU VALUE?

What do you love doing every day that doesn't require much motivation? Sometimes we place value on things that are not important to us. There are numerous stories of people who choose careers based on what is acceptable rather than what is aligned with their core values and what they would love to do. It is only later in life that they experience deep regret and wish they could have chosen otherwise for themselves.

Those who believe in the importance of pursuing what they value and take inspired action to achieve their goals often flourish. Become unique individuals who walk the earth proudly, authentically, and with a joyful heart, knowing that they gave themselves a fair chance to achieve their goals and dreams in life. J.K. Rowling, the author of the Harry Potter series, did not stop writing her stories of young wizards who attended a magical school called Hogwarts when she faced setbacks. She believed in the importance of her work and pursued what her heart called her to achieve.

She had a whole stack of reasons to stop writing and work in an unsatisfying job that limited her potential to become a legendary author. She was broke, living in poverty, struggling to pay her rent, divorced, and a single mother. She was also rejected by all of the major publishing companies in Britain when she first submitted her first book in the Harry Potter series. However, she did not give up, and all it took was one little person to love her book, which led to the first 500 *Harry Potter And The Philosophers Stone* being sold. The first young reader was the daughter of the head of Bloomsbury Publishing.

In Chapter 4, I mentioned how important it was to ask ourselves powerful questions. Well, it is just as important to reply with powerful answers. A powerful solution nudges you into an unknown possibility that you were initially afraid of pursuing because you felt you were not good enough. A powerful answer is the most accurate answer you can offer yourself from your heart. Ask yourself if you were given a chance to paint a picture of the most purposeful and personally rewarding life you would love to live; what would that be?

Such as Dr. John Demartini, once a homeless high-school dropout who travels the world 365 days a year to teach and heal people from their limitations and mental challenges. He often says, "When the vision on the inside is louder than all the opinions on the outside, you have begun to master your life." What you value in life and where you place your energy matter. The vision you hold in your heart for your life, based on an earnest desire to pursue it, does matter. You will do an impressive job if you know what you value, believe in it, and are willing to take inspired action.

REASONS TO ALIGN YOUR CORE VALUES WITH YOUR GOALS

When you give yourself enough reasons to align your core values with your goals, this chapter will provide you with more reasons to consider choosing authentic plans that meet the criteria of your core values. Many wise, world-renowned philosophers and human behavior experts have changed the lives of millions of people by revealing an eternal truth that has set them free.

Their wisdom is contained in these few words, "Do what you love, and love what you do." It is a simple philosophy that can be traced back to the first philosophers who made their wisdom known, like Greek philosophers Aristotle and Plato, who both lived in the 6th and 7th centuries BC. These magic words are widely accepted as the eternal truth of what it means to live a life of purpose and true wealth. Simply choosing to do what you love is a choice that is reflective of what it means to live a life that is full of meaning, purposeful encounters, and magical manifestations of what you value the most in life.

According to Plato, the meaning of life is linked to a unique purpose, which in turn is the path to attaining the highest form of "self" (Modi, 2021). In other words, finding meaning in life is the path that leads us to self-realization and self-actualization. You have to look around you to notice the collective accomplishments of human beings. All these things we see around us are the accomplishments of people seeking self-fulfillment through purpose and innovation. These accomplishments have solved many of our global challenges and mutual problems.

It may not necessarily be one thing that inspires you, but a collection of ideas that may be connected to a few core values. For example, if you feel purposeful when making a social difference in your community, your core value, "to make a difference," could be linked to a social cause. Once you link your goals to a social reason that feels right for you, there will most likely be many paths that can lead you to achieve your end goal: To make a meaningful difference.

You have to look around you and channel your energies to find a path that resonates the most with how you would love to actualize your purpose or social mission. The simple idea behind this wisdom–do what you love–is to honor what is sacred and vital to you— what ticks all the boxes for you, makes your heart sing with joy, and allows you the freedom to explore your creative talents in all areas of deep personal interest.

Life is usually good when the things you do and the way you behave match your values. Life may not always be peachy, but setting out to find a higher calling linked to your core values, will be the best gift of personal empowerment you can give yourself. When things don't align with our values, they feel wrong for us, which often leads to feelings of frustration, inadequacy, or a sense of being "lost in the world."

Here are 10 reasons to focus on setting goals that you would love to achieve in your lifetime and that are comfortably aligned with your values:

You weren't born to just pay the bills. We all intrinsically accept that we do not merely work to pay the bills. We are social and creative beings. Therefore, finding meaningful work is the cherry on top of the cake. Why spend a large portion of your life working to earn a living when you may feel that you're in the wrong job or profession? Choose work that inspires you from within, as this will give you more reason to expand and grow personally and professionally.

You will be more productive. You will most likely be more productive and fully engaged in your daily tasks when you are inspired from within and go the extra mile to achieve fulfillment in your work.

Your motivation levels will naturally be higher. You will also feel more ambitious about your prospects and aspire to tremendous success in all areas of your life. The feeling of success is contagious, and achieving success at work will rub off on all other areas of your life.

You will feel more purposeful and therefore fulfilled. When you feel good about your work, you will feel great about who you are and where you are going. You will want to wake up in the mornings ready to achieve great things and meet amazing, like-minded people on the same mission as you.

Your work will not feel like a chore. When you love what you're doing, your work will feel worth the effort and time you put into it. You will love thinking about it and enjoy contributing over and beyond your primary functions.

You will push yourself to succeed even more. The more you achieve fulfillment in your work, the higher your chances are of pushing yourself to grow beyond your current job. You will naturally aim for higher achievements and excel in your career.

You have more reason to expand your skills and learning outcomes. You will experience great motivation to keep learning, growing, and expanding in knowledge, thereby becoming a leader in your own right.

You will feel good about serving others who require your skills. This is what feeling purposeful is all about, being in a position to serve others who recognize your interest, skills, and passion.

You will be willing to face challenges head-on and see them as opportunities instead of setbacks. You've got to love what you do because you will undoubtedly face challenges, setbacks, and even failure. When you love what you do, it will fuel you to keep going and learning. Failure and setbacks will be signals to learn more extraordinary things or to come up with new creative ideas to improve your chances of success.

You will feel great knowing that you overcame self-limiting beliefs to achieve your greatest potential. Finally, all the effort you put into living a meaningful, purposeful life will be worth it in the end. There will be no regrets, only memories worth reflecting on and achievements worth celebrating (Vishnuverma48, 2016).

VALUES CAN CHANGE

As we identify our values and align them confidently with what we love doing, we should be aware of a universal fact of life, "The only constant is change." We should be moving forward, not backward; therefore, appreciating that values need to change over time is vital when setting goals. The ongoing process of self-reflection for change is moving forward as we progress in our unique journeys to experience interesting new junctures in our personal and professional lives.

Our values also depend on how we evolve as individual beings. When we start in life, we may have an idea of what we would love to do in pursuit of a particular career after seeing others succeed. We may be inspired to learn a skill set because it is relevant to finding work based on the value of "Grit." With this value, we may choose to empower ourselves to earn a living.

As we expand and grow into unique individuals, inspiration is bound to shift our values in new directions. When this happens, we will also most likely have a change of heart about what we value most in life. For example, your value could have shifted from "Grit" to "Creativity." This could've sparked entrepreneurial interests, and you may have decided that you would love to turn your hobby into a lucrative business venture.

At other times, a change in values can occur when we reach critical new milestones or turning points in our lives, such as retirement. These turning points give us new opportunities to evaluate what is truly important to us. Sometimes we can also feel overwhelmed about these changes occurring, especially when we need to spend more time self-reflecting and assessing the change that presents itself to us.

This is why goal-setting and asking ourselves honest questions about what is going on in our lives should be an ongoing process. Having a master plan in place for your life will enable you to constantly evaluate what is working, what isn't working anymore, and what needs to be modified or changed to suit an ever-evolving life.

As we begin our journey into goal setting for the short, medium, and long term, remember that nothing is cast in stone. Everything is changeable and relevant as long as it is essential to us. When things that were once important to us are no longer relevant, it is time to let go, value the journey behind them, cherish the learning that has taken place, and honor our achievements. We decide on what new things and activities we would love to engage in and what would be the most inspiring plan of action to take.

LEARNING-BASED ACTION

Identifying Your Values

Do not skip this exercise as we identify our values in all critical areas of what we value in life. This will undoubtedly assist us in setting authentic and relevant goals.

Without identifying what we value in life, not seeing that deep inside us, we are capable of much more than what we give credit to ourselves.

This is where the magic happens; you will direct your mind in preparing your subconscious to know that this is how you will create your new life. Let's get started in identifying what you value the most in life.

Step 1

Grab your pen and journal, or open your Master Plan for Life document on your PC or Laptop and go to Chapter 5. If you have not downloaded your digital copy, click or copy and paste the link or go to **https://go.f4ury.com/knowing-what-you-think-about-is-where-you-will-go** to place you in a position to give yourself the upper hand to value what you love doing in each area of your life.

Step 2

Go to chapter 4 in steps 2 and 4, where you've listed the core beliefs in each area of your life and converted your limiting belief into an unlimited one.

Step 3

List all your values in all areas of your life.

For example, when it comes to Finance, your core value may be to achieve *Financial Independence* (that is a value).

This means that you are placing a high value on *Financial Independence* as opposed to earning a salary.

You could also place a high value on *Creativity*. This is an important indicator that you would love to engage in work that will raise your level of creativity and see you on your way to becoming *Financially Independent.*

Step 4

Values help us establish clarity on the kinds of goals we would love to pursue.

Start making a list of the goals you would love to achieve in each area of your life.

For example, in pursuit of the value of achieving *Financial independence*, you could list a goal of creating a new entrepreneurial venture based on your hobby, which will also match up to the value that you place on increasing *Creativity*.

Step 5

Once you've completed the list, go over them again to make sure that your values are absolutely authentic.

When you clearly identify what you value in life, you have just started to become aware and get a different perspective on how your life can be created. Once you've completed this exercise, you are ready to move on to the next powerful chapter, where we will set up the ultimate goal plan.

Here you will be given the opportunity to create a roadmap of success, reminding yourself that this is how you will reach your final destination toward achieving your goals.

6

SETTING UP THE ULTIMATE GOAL PLAN

> *If you don't know where you are going, you'll end up someplace else.*
>
> — YOGI BERRA

MAKE A PLAN THAT YOU CAN STICK WITH

When you decide that life is worth living to the fullest and that your dreams, goals, and accomplishments matter, the next step is committing to success. Our subconscious mind needs to be programmed with this mindset firmly in place. Since you've come this far and have taken significant steps toward eliminating the limiting beliefs, you have identified what is holding you back. You are ready and consciously aware of how important it is to consistently groom your mind with thoughts that empower your dreams and goals.

Committing to your success should be directed at identifying YOUR ideas of success. Drawing up a plan of action that you can stick with 365 days a year will further empower your subconscious mind to make the commitment necessary to achieve your goals. Your ultimate goal plan is your blueprint for success and will help you achieve absolute clarity in your vision. The person you will become after reaching the summit of your success will astound you.

You are setting out to achieve growth by learning and developing yourself to pursue success. You will revolutionize from within what magically resonates with the identity of what success means to you. However, we must be willing to climb the mountain for 365 days a year to get what we want out of life. Your ultimate goal plan is different from setting new year's resolutions. It is not your wish list but a strategic plan outlining the action steps you must be willing to take each day.

Do not look at days as time; look at a day as soon as you wake up and until you go to sleep. At the end of each, you need to be in a position to pat yourself on the back for taking one or a few more significant steps toward achieving the long, medium, and short-term goals you will now create in this chapter. It is essential to complete tasks each day that are aligned with your long and medium-term goals. The effort you put into your daily tasks should count the most. If you complete one small task a day and are consistent, you will have completed 365 small tasks in a year.

This can be related to any personal or professional goal that you have in mind. It can be as simple as waking up earlier, cleaning the house, mowing the lawn, working on your relationships, completing a course, reading a book, improving your fitness, or starting a business. It doesn't matter how big or small the goal is; what matters is your ability to achieve it within your timeline. Breaking down your goal setting is crucial when creating the ultimate goal plan so that even the micro daily goals end up supporting the new lifestyle pushing you to reach the summit of your success.

THE IMPORTANCE OF GOAL SETTING

It is essential to understand why we must set goals for ourselves. We already established in Chapter 4 that to achieve learning, part of the process involves closing gaps that prevent us from experiencing ultimate growth, thus reprogramming your brain's neurological connection. There are more reasons attached to setting life-long transformational goals. Here are some to reflect upon in your life journey.

You take control of your life. When we do not set specific goals but fantasize about the life we wish to live ultimately, we plan to remain in fantasies. To achieve success, we must take control of what we do each day to ensure that we consistently live the life of our dreams by following rituals that help us achieve significant milestones, growth, and new skills.

You create direction in your work. Having a plan and sticking to it within the expected timelines set against each goal gives you clear direction in your work. This means there's hardly a chance of remaining stuck in one position throughout your life. As long as you keep moving forward in new exciting directions, you will progress consistently, grow, and expand in knowledge and skills. You will also widen your outlook even further than when you began your journey—ensuring that you remain aligned with the most meaningful things.

You will be authentic, as opposed to letting other people run your life. No one wakes up every morning dedicated to the things that make YOUR life meaningful. Each person prioritizes what is important to them, not you. To be the captain of your ship, you will need a plan to get you to the destination you wish to reach in life. The captain should know how to steer his ship and refrain from allowing others to take over, as this will reduce the likelihood of arriving on time at your destination.

You will feel fulfilled from within, and confident about your abilities. No one can make you feel fulfilled from within and confident as much as you can. If you are stuck on feeling you are not good enough to achieve your goals, YOU can only eliminate this feeling. As you've discovered already, eliminating limiting beliefs requires that you do the work from within yourself. When you are on fire and believe in yourself, any milestone achieved that is aligned with your goals will further fuel you to achieve more and more.

STEPS TO CREATING UNIQUE GOALS

Here are simple steps to help you create unique goals that are worthy of your time, effort, and attention.

Ask yourself what the end result is that you would love to achieve. To begin our journey, we must start with the end in mind. If you love to occupy your time making a valuable difference in a social cause, for example, then consider what that contribution should look like in full color, and even imagine your entire life's contribution playing out in a fully imagined movie in your mind.

Determine what is required of you to achieve the goal. Your next step would be to determine the line of action that will be required of you throughout your life to achieve the end goal that you have just envisioned for yourself. Write it down in point form, and you will be able to elaborate on each goal as you work through your ultimate goal plan.

Ask yourself how it will make you feel to achieve those goals. This is a crucial step to take when achieving clarity. Usually, we select goals that feel right for us. To ascertain with clarity whether these goals that we are setting are indeed right for us, we need to ask ourselves how it will make us feel to achieve those goals.

Are these goals worth the effort on your part? Remember, if you don't love what you do, the chances of frustrating yourself in the attempt to achieve your goals remain pretty high. Ask yourself if the goals you have set will, according to your current frame of reference, be worth the effort you are going to pour into them.

Are you willing to spend long hours working toward their fulfillment? Make sure that you are excited about the prospect of achieving your goals. Planning to put in the long hours necessary to reach the summit of your success requires dedication, commitment, and perseverance. Also, remember that life is not all smooth sailing. You will face setbacks, challenges, and even some failures. Remember that setbacks and failures are only learning opportunities to achieve total success.

If you've hesitated in the past to initiate a plan of action, ask yourself why. Be honest now with yourself as you step into the powerful process of designing the ultimate goal plan for your life. Have you hesitated to initiate a plan of action around the same desired vision, and if so, why? Also, ask yourself if you have now resolved those issues, and if not, how you plan to resolve these outstanding issues that may still be standing in the way.

Ask yourself if you are feeling unfulfilled at present because you have not undertaken to achieve the goals that are most meaningful to you. This step presents an excellent opportunity to examine the current level of personal fulfillment you are experiencing in your life. Realize that it is imperative that you go ahead and create this fantastic blueprint for your life to improve your chances of feeling considerably fulfilled from within.

Will you have more regrets later in life for not pursuing your goals and dreams? Answer honestly and bluntly if you foresee yourself having any regrets later in life if you continue down the current trajectory. Have you set yourself up for success with the ambitious, inspiring new trajectory to create growth personally or professionally?

How do you feel about taking a new journey into the unknown world of possibilities? Now is the time to establish any sense of excitement that you are feeling as you contemplate stepping away from mediocrity and into the realm of unknown possibilities and limitlessness. If you're excited and slightly nervous, you're ready to change your life and set long-, medium-, and short-term goals to get your mind to start visualizing your future and being creative.

LONG-TERM GOAL SETTING

Consider what you would love to achieve within 5–10 years from now, and make a list. Make sure you list everything, then start examining each one to see if you can group them into the following categories:

Health Goals. Here is where you set a positive tone, especially concerning your health. You will feel good physically and mentally, as it takes you toward long-term benefits, increasing the emphasis on promoting a healthy lifestyle to prevent diseases. Here are some examples to get started; you may begin a fitness program and be more mindful of eating the best nutritious foods to stay healthy by eating healthier, being physically active, maintaining a healthy weight, and sleeping better.

Family/Relationship Goals. Relationship goals are an essential part of our lives; naturally, we would love to set goals to make them meaningful. Here are some examples to consider: increase family time, get married, get in a relationship, have children, communicate more with your partner, and not take people for granted.

Career Goals. Consider aligning your goals with your qualities and professional experience to provide an adequate response. For example, if you're in an entry-level position, your goal may include how you can advance into a leadership position and the steps. It may also include what skills you need to acquire to be relevant in the marketplace or, if entrepreneurship may be something of interest, what skills are needed to make this happen.

Financial Goals. When developing a financial goal, it is best to aim at the target when managing your money. It can easily involve earning, investing, saving, or spending. Working towards your target is easy when you clearly understand what you're aiming for. An example of a goal may include building a retirement fund, creating an emergency savings account, paying off debt, investing in assets, or finding a higher-paying job.

Educational Goals. Education is a broad field; it does not just mean returning to school to get a higher level of education. You can include examples such as personal development growth, attending an online seminar, or reading books in your area of interest that you would love to improve personally or professionally. When describing your educational goals, what qualifications and talents do you feel you must have for your career field? Include in your plans for financing your education to include individual aspirations of the competencies, skills, and qualities you will acquire after completing a program or course.

Spiritual and Wellness Goals. A spiritual goal can help us thrive personally if we follow a particular religion or someone spiritual but not religious. Some examples may include attending church regularly, being more mindful, meditating daily, volunteering periodically, showing more compassion, or donating money to your favorite charity.

Lifestyle Goals. Identify your overall goal of how you would love to live. Here we are looking at your ambitions to live your dream life. This may include the house you would love to have, the cars, and the freedom to spend more time with family and friends, to live and work wherever your heart desires. How would it feel to have the ability to live out your true dreams, and how will you achieve this?

Now that you've completed making changes in the areas of your life when reviewing your Master Plan for Life Journal, we are currently adding layers to this process to help you achieve clarity. We are also becoming more specific about the goals we want to accomplish within this long-term range. Once you have listed your long-term goals, add reference points for when you believe they are going to happen. Do not worry about how you will get there.

Remember, this is your big "why," the long-term vision statement of your goals to turn them into reality. No matter where you are at currently, be bold and think big for each category that adequately describes what you want and when you believe it will be achieved. For example, "I will create a thriving business venture out of my hobby of making unique vintage teddy bears by selling them online and distributing them to major local retailers or worldwide. I will also hire local talent, thus empowering skilled people with a chance to contribute meaningfully to the growth of my organization."

MEDIUM-TERM GOAL SETTING

Then reflect on your big long-term vision and think about what you are willing to do within 1 to 3 years. Then group your goals into specific categories for each goal. This time you will break it down further from your long to medium-term goals, linking the two together. You will build momentum toward a measurable result within this period by visualizing that it has already happened and when you believe it will happen.

Follow with a medium-term vision statement for each category of goals that will adequately describe the purpose of its full attainment within the allocated time frame. For example, "I will create a unique collection of vintage teddy bears. It would best serve me to use my talent to creatively develop unique designs of vintage teddy bears to appeal to teddy bear lovers, collectors, and local consumers. Who wishes to create magical experiences in gift offerings or decorate their children's rooms with beautiful, unique teddy bears currently unavailable in the market?"

SHORT-TERM GOAL SETTING

This is the perfect time to look at your current situation and determine what you will do to achieve your goals within the next 3–6 months. Given your current position regarding these goals, these goals must be realistic and achievable. Now list all of your short-term goals, and allocate a time frame for accomplishing your goals related to your medium-term goals.

Finally, write a short-term vision statement for each category of goals you intend to achieve within this time frame. For example, "I will perfect the art of teddy bear making and will research to see what is currently on the market. The goal will be to experiment and research new techniques during this timeline. I aim to create two new, unique-looking teddy bears. Make teddy bears that stand out uniquely from the market and take teddy bear-making fun to new levels of personal enjoyment."

ONCE THE GOAL IS MADE, WHAT NEXT?

Make sure you have support from your family, friends, and significant relationships. This will ensure that you plan personal time for family and close friends. Keep a healthy balance between work and play. Remember not to overdo things. Embrace the journey to stay healthy, vibrant, and focused instead of working yourself into the ground.

This is why it is essential to have a support system and follow a self-care routine to keep you feeling positively inspired, healthy, and loved. The purpose of having short-term goals in your line of sight is to ensure that you are consistently chunking down your goals into measurable and achievable milestones and manageable steps. Be realistic and practical in how you set out to achieve your short-term goals every day, one step at a time.

Remember that your goals will require constant attention, modification, and tweaks as you assess what is and isn't working. The beauty of setting long, medium, and short-term goals is that you will constantly be reminding your subconscious of your big long-term vision, causing it to begin reprogramming itself to accept this new reality in advance.

As we progress in our journey together, we learn how important it is to achieve a healthy balance in our lives and that we can achieve harmony with a fair amount of effort without neglecting any area of our lives or essential relationships with others—working smart by working hard but not at the expense of your health or relationships.

HOW TO PRODUCE ACTIONABLE RESULTS

Start slow and start with one task you will complete daily. When you have developed the habit of completing a daily task, you can add more of what you need to complete. When you are consistently comfortable, add two more daily tasks by challenging yourself to add more, and so on. The idea is to keep our tasks consistent while challenging them simultaneously. When we are challenged, we grow.

For example, if one of your goals is to improve your fitness level, start walking for a month. After that, you can increase your daily goal by adding more distance or changing the route to a slightly more challenging one. Alternately, you can slowly incorporate jogging into your routine, and daily you do more to achieve milestones along the way of achieving your medium and long-term goals. Then, doing the math will give you a bigger picture of how quickly a goal can be completed in a year.

For instance, if you are consistent, you will have completed 1095 small daily tasks in one year if no problems or delays occur. This is when you have completed three small daily tasks and how you can manipulate time and your subconscious to achieve your goal much faster. When you look at completing a task in one day, time does not matter. Nothing should matter when you focus on meeting the scheduled task for that day.

REVIEW YOUR PLAN IN THE EVENING AND CHECK OFF TASKS THAT WERE COMPLETED

Make accountability for your day's progress a vital part of ensuring that you stay on track, one goal at a time. When reviewing your daily plan every evening, remind yourself of your "why" to remain accountable to yourself and your purpose. You are reprogramming your life by doing your best to achieve each day's task. Do not worry; if a task is not met, no sweat; that task will be the next day's priority. The other reason for reviewing your list every evening, you will begin to teach your subconscious while you sleep how to stay on track with your ultimate goal plan when you wake up the next day.

Remind yourself that you are the CEO of your life and the importance of planning the following day's events to complete what you intended for one day.

Remember to celebrate small milestones as you progress to build momentum. Also, it is a healthy way of validating your efforts with a constant commitment toward reaching your goals. Rewards will keep us inspired in the long term and remind us that our efforts are paying off.

LEARNING-BASED ACTION

Creating the Ultimate Goal Plan: Taking Action

This entire chapter is dedicated to ensuring that you have created your long-, medium-, and short-term goals and a daily task list that can be implemented immediately. Here you must be vigilant to clearly state and identify how you would love to live out your goals and aspirations to live the best life.

This will be the stepping stone where you take inspired action to realize your dreams to set up the ultimate goal plan for your subconscious mind to accept the new reality you will be creating. Additionally, this is how you can actualize the desired outcome and the willingness to make the necessary sacrifices to achieve your goals.

Step 1

Grab your pen and journal, or open your Master Plan for Life document on your PC or Laptop and go to Chapter 6. If you have not downloaded your digital copy, click or copy and paste the link or go to **https://go.f4ury.com/knowing-what-you-think-about-is-where-you-will-go** to start working on your ultimate goal plan to set a system in place for you to be able to achieve your life long goals.

Step 2

Ask yourself these questions when referring to your goals:

- What is the result you would love to achieve?
- What is required of you to achieve your goals?
- How will it make you feel to achieve your goals?
- Are these goals worth the effort?
- Are you prepared to spend long hours working toward their fulfillment?
- If you have hesitated in the past to initiate action, ask yourself why.

- Are you feeling unfulfilled at present and correlating this feeling to these goals not being achieved?
- Will you have more regrets in life if you do not pursue the fulfillment of these goals?
- Are these goals worth the effort on your part?
- Are you excited and slightly nervous about taking this journey into unknown possibilities?

Step 3

Prepare your long-term goals concisely and precisely as set out in this chapter, read over them, and contemplate this vision by picturing their full attainment.

Step 4

Prepare your medium-term goals concisely and precisely as set out in this chapter, read over them, and contemplate this vision by picturing their full attainment.

Step 5

Prepare your short-term goals concisely and precisely as set out in this chapter, read over them, and contemplate this vision by picturing their full attainment.

Step 6

Finally, draw up a daily task section, start listing what you currently do daily, and amend it by removing anything that is not positively aligned with your goals. Such as time wasted binge-watching on Netflix, television, news, social media, hanging out with friends, or anything not related that is not empowering you in your area of interest.

Step 7

Create a list of new activities to incorporate into your daily routine aligned with your long-term, medium-term, and short-term goals.

———

Now that you have set up your short-, medium- and long-term goals, you are ready to move on to the next phase of goal setting. In Chapter 7, we will create purposeful mornings to see everything that you desire on the way. Setting your ultimate goal plan will always begin with how your morning begins. This will set the stage for achieving your goals in the long run.

7

CREATING PURPOSEFUL
MORNINGS

> *This is not just another day, this is yet another chance to make your dreams come true.*
>
> — UNKNOWN

How you start your day, knowing where you're going, will determine its success. Maybe yesterday was not so great, or the day before was even worse. But you're here now, and you've started this inspiring journey to take your life to a new level of insight, growth, productivity, and joy. Freedom will be yours when you follow a structured path to uplift you. As radical as it may sound, the structure is a blessing, especially when you intentionally create the life you want.

Without goals, we will pointlessly engage in events with no meaning, finding ourselves stuck in never-ending cycles of frustration, mundanity, mediocrity, and self-defeat. On the other hand, when we set meaningful goals for ourselves, we reaffirm our belief that we are worthy of living inspiring, purposeful lives. Now that you have long-term, medium-term, and short-term goals in place, it is time to adopt a structured approach to your mornings to ensure that success does not remain an elusive thing but an everyday conscious choice that we make in our process of how we start our day's journey.

Our approach to our mornings needs to energize us, putting us directly in touch with all we value from waking to a brand-new day. The slate is clean every morning, waiting for a paintbrush to splash bright colors onto the blank canvas awaiting your creative genius. Still, deciding to paint your day depends on the picture you hold in your mind and what to paint. Your entire day can become more intentional and less chaotic when you determine the outcome in advance. We control how our day progresses, from the moment we awake until we go to bed to rest our bodies, minds, and souls.

As you already know, when we step out of bed on the wrong foot, our days can also feel out of control as we carry that negative energy throughout the day. On the other hand, if we start our days off right, feeling energized from within and having moments to be grateful for our days, they can fly by with productivity. You decide on the type of day you would love to have. You also decide on your reactions to stressful situations. Creating a purposeful morning can be an amazing gift to give yourself daily.

THE WAKING MIND AND PHASES

Sleep Inertia and the Effects of Waking Up

Just watching the sunrise while sipping your favorite morning brew and enjoying the cool breeze will revitalize you and inspire you to awaken to another good day. Therefore, getting excited about the goals you will begin to pursue will enable you to be enthused for the day, which presents new opportunities to grow and expand in the direction of your goals. When you know where you are going, every sunrise provides enough excitement and the awe of a new beginning to do what you love.

In reality, all mornings won't be perfect. Some of us do experience sleep inertia, which is normal. Being aware of sleep inertia can prepare you for any momentary lapses of morning stress when you want to stay in bed, groggy, and slightly disoriented. Sleep inertia is a common effect of morning grogginess. It usually only lasts for a short time. A cup of morning coffee can do the trick to get you wired up and purposeful. However, you can only sometimes count on coffee to give you the quick perk-up you need.

Sometimes, all we need is a refreshing glass of water with a dash of lemon on the side is more effective. Or how about a quick jog around the block to refresh your body, mind, and soul? Getting fresh air in the morning by stepping outside is a good antidote for sleep inertia, and there are so many other activities in your morning routine to start your day on the right side.

If you experience excessive sleep, inertia, and struggle, these could be linked to the activities you engaged in the night prior. Try relaxing more and clearing your mind before you retire to bed, or engage in guided sleep meditations to ensure that you are completely relaxed and stress-free as you fall asleep. You can find plenty of sleep relaxation music and guided meditations on YouTube.

There would naturally be those nights when you end up working until the early parts of the morning. This is perfectly acceptable. When your work schedule tends to increase in proportion to healthy challenges aligned with your goals, it is natural to work harder at times.

Schedule quality rest when this happens to ensure you live a well-balanced, healthy lifestyle to ensure maximum wellness and optimal productivity. Trust your intuition and listen to your body when it communicates with you. Even though a certain amount of sleep inertia is normal, grogginess that lasts more than a few minutes in the morning may relate to symptoms that need further analysis. When this occurs, consult a medical doctor or a sleep therapist (Dasgupta, 2020).

Hacks to Fighting Morning Fatigue

Here are more solutions to encourage you to shake off those slow, sluggish starts to the day.

Don't hit snooze at all. It's easier said than done when we've programmed our minds to accept waking up later, relying on the snooze button to work our way out of the morning blues. However, waking up at least 15 minutes earlier than usual makes all the difference when you're on purpose. If you're having trouble waking up on time, try setting your alarm for 90 minutes before you aim to rise and shine instead of hitting the snooze button to reprogram your subconscious mind after your targeted wake-up time.

Drink a glass of water first thing. Starting your day with a healthy glass of fresh water is what your body needs to stimulate healthy thoughts and mindful habits. Drinking water throughout the day will provide a source of life and vitality. You can add a slice of lemon, cucumber, or strawberry to keep you inspired and motivated.

Splash your face with water. Splash your face with water when you awake, and see how refreshing that feels. You can also try icing your face by rubbing a cube in circular motions. This will wake you up and add a refreshing, cool touch while reducing puffiness around your eyes and cheeks.

Stretch out your tired body with yoga. Yoga is a wonderful way to incorporate mindful meditation and gentle exercises that will awaken your muscles. Yoga can naturally inspire you to stay healthy in your thoughts and actions. Yoga also boosts your energy levels and is known to improve the functioning of your brain.

Energize your body with a healthy breakfast. You don't have to opt for a heavy breakfast with fried foods; that will make you feel more lethargic. Instead, stick to fresh fruit, a slice of whole grain toast, or energizing spreads like peanut or almond butter. Always opt for healthier choices as your first meal of the day. You will get that bounce back in your step and won't regret making healthier choices.

Avoid having sugar in the mornings. Avoid a sugary start to your day. Sugar can cause the classic blood sugar spike and leave you feeling drained later. Opt for fresh juices and get the sugar out of your coffee. Water is still your best choice, especially on an empty stomach. Sip water throughout your morning workouts.

Go outside to activate your brain. An even better choice is to get your morning stretches done outside. A quick jog, fresh air, and stretches will improve your chances of developing long-term healthier morning habits, improving health, fitness, and your zest for life.

Get some cardio exercise. A morning booster is a quick 10 to 30-minute cardio exercise routine. It will energize you and boost your heart rate, oxygenating your cells. Think about your goals for the day as you start your day on a high note with a high or low-impact cardio workout. For some people, a morning cardio session is highly motivating and fun.

Address your stress. Make sure to manage your morning stress levels by preparing as much as possible the night before, like your children's school lunch or going over their homework. Also, ensure that your work things are appropriately arranged in advance, like your briefcase, laptop, and other significant work items, as well as your clothing. Rushing about in the morning to get things done can create unnecessary stress and anxiety. Be organized.

Give yourself something to look forward to. Plan something special you would love to do in the mornings to increase your confidence and boost your morale. How about a morning podcast that inspires you or a morning social call with a dear friend to keep you motivated and inspired? (Garone, 2020)

Setting the Stage With Easy Morning Routines

A healthy, focused morning routine sets a low-stress tone for the whole day. You don't even have to go by what the experts are saying. Shift your morning routine to a more inspiring start to support your state of wellness; you will naturally benefit from the fantastic results, as so many others have. Here are some examples of how famous, successful people start their days.

Oprah Winfrey

World-renowned talk show host Oprah Winfrey loves watching nature from her bedroom window when she wakes up in the mornings. Watching wild geese fly over her backyard is her favorite morning activity. She also enjoys looking at the ocean view and soaking in everything about nature. She then brushes her teeth, takes the dogs out, and makes some coffee.

While her coffee is brewing, she meditates. While enjoying her coffee, Oprah reads five cards from her "365 Gathered Truths" box. At 9 a.m., Oprah begins her morning exercise routine. After stretching her body and doing a low-impact workout, she also enjoys running around her property (Ellis, 2021).

Deepak Chopra

Deepak Chopra is a world-renowned spiritual leader. Authored 64 books, of which 19 are bestsellers. Every day, he starts his day at 6 a.m., beginning with 90 minutes of mindful meditation. Then, with his ritual of drinking three cups of black coffee, he justifies his coffee fixation based on its powerful antioxidant benefits. Unsurprisingly, his daily routine also involves yoga.

Sometimes he does it alone, while other times, he prefers to be guided by a teacher. The rest of the day consists of writing, eating light vegetarian meals, and walking. Deepak says his routine doesn't break; it bends. He allows for flexibility depending on his schedule but sticks to his routine most of the time. He still maintains a similar schedule if he's traveling or on vacation. Deepak does take weekends off for rest and family time (The Optimist Daily, 2019).

Bill Gates

Bill Gates, an American business magnate, software developer, investor, author, and philanthropist, starts his day in his private gym. Here, he spends an hour in the mornings on the treadmill, all while watching; DVDs from the Teaching Company's "Great Courses" series. After that, he catches up with the headlines from around the world. His favorite topics include public health policy. Bill follows a very similar routine to Elon Musk, the wealthiest man on earth. They both tend to break down their daily schedules into five-minute intervals (Grind, 2021).

CREATE YOUR OWN MORNING PLAN

Now that I've given you some inspiring ideas to kick-start your day, you are ready to create your morning plan. Keep in mind that the structure you choose must feel right for you. Repeating your purposeful morning routine is essential to program your subconscious mind accordingly. Remember that 66 days without breaking it to develop a new morning routine will allow your brain to adjust according to your subconscious mind. Soon it will be your new habit, and you will reach out every morning to do the things you love to get your day off to a great start.

Now that you have many purposeful morning ideas in this chapter, below are more suggested morning ideas to assist you in structuring your mornings based on your preferences. Before ticking them off, please go through them to decide which works best for you. When starting, you can experiment with new ideas to see whether they work for you. Consider alternating some activities and adding variety to spice up your mornings, making them adventurous, exciting, and purposeful.

Also, review your daily plans in the evenings to ensure that you attend to your new morning routine of taking care of yourself first, especially on days that may be busier than others. Sometimes you may need to wake up earlier and plan your time better to ensure you don't miss the most vital part of your day. You can decide on the best time to plan your next morning—usually, the evenings work great as you would have a clearer idea of your immediate priorities for the next day.

Make a plan to give your morning a purposeful boost. Developing a daily morning routine isn't about adding more to your plate. With a solid morning plan, you will naturally give yourself more energy during the day, brightening your mood while boosting your productivity, reducing anxiety, and making you feel better overall. You can give yourself an inspiring boost of motivation by simply making positive changes—be amazed at how your entire day will shift to you achieving so much more.

Wake up earlier. During the waking moments of the morning, your mind will be less inclined to overthink and can naturally do things. It allows you to absorb more information when you wake; you can be fully alert and focused due to the brain chemistry at that time. You might even get some insight or inspiration. You will give yourself the time without distraction to focus on the things that matter for the day. Instead of getting up late and rushing through your schedule before you even begin. Experiment with what works best for you. And it might mean waking up earlier can benefit your overall success.

Drink water. The benefits of drinking water are tremendous. Water is vital for the proper functioning of all our vital organs and removes toxins from our bodies. Staying hydrated remains one of the wisest choices to make for ourselves. Drinking water in the morning will increase your energy levels. Water allows for an increase in red blood cell count, and by increasing the oxygen supply, we receive more oxygen to the brain. The rise in oxygen will create more wakefulness and energy so that you can start your morning off right. Keep some water at your bedside so you are sure not to miss out on your first glass of water when you wake up.

Meditate. Meditation is the customary process of training your mind to refocus and redirect your thoughts toward what is important to you. Theoretical research studies all indicate that practicing meditation and mindfulness regularly can change brain activity.

Many people, just like me, have practiced developing its beneficial habits, and I can therefore vouch for the shifts that occur during meditation sessions. It's resulted in creating a positive mood, outlook, and self-discipline. A significant advantage of meditation includes reducing stress and anxiety while promoting a healthier emotional balance.

Journal new ideas. From scientific geniuses to artists and everyone in between, keeping a journal can serve as a self-care tool and will keep you on track with all your brilliant ideas, thoughts, and emotions. Journaling can help you track progress and growth, gain self-confidence, improve your writing and communication skills, and find inspirational insights that come to your mind. How we feel about our ideas is just as important as simply noting them down. Journaling is a fun way of also improving your relationship and communication with yourself.

Exercise. When creating your ultimate goal plan, staying physically active is just as important. You will automatically improve your brain function, enabling you to think clearly, manage your weight, reduce the risk of disease, strengthen bones and muscles, and improve your everyday activities. Primarily when you are out to achieve and win in life, exercise can really boost how you feel about yourself, and in the mornings, it's a great energy enhancer.

Get Some Sun. Getting your morning dose of sunlight is essential for the health and well-being of your mental state and helps you naturally produce vitamin D. Research also indicates that getting natural light in the morning will assist in you sleeping better at night. However, we all know how wonderful it feels when we did catch those first rays of morning sunshine on some occasions. Make it a habit, and embrace your cosmic existence with the sun's healing rays (Peterson, n.d.).

Stretching. Consider stretching first thing in the morning to relieve any tension or pains from the night before. You will help your body to increase its blood flow and prepare you for the day ahead by stimulating your blood flow while relaxing your muscles and bringing fluidity to your movements. Stretching will awaken your body and leave you feeling aligned physically. Mentally, it is a cathartic experience—a meditative connection with your body.

Morning Gratitude. Gratitude is described as the state of being grateful. It involves expressing gratitude for appreciating something, from a gift to life. This can range from seeing a beautiful flower to witnessing the sunrise or sunset—or even giving thanks for recovering from a severe illness or an accomplishment. Regular practice can have measurable positive effects on your life and health. You will boost your immune system, improve relationships, and increase optimism.

Music. It was Shakespeare who famously said, "If music is the food of love, play on!" No truer words could have been spoken. Whatever type of music inspires you, use it in your workout, or just listen to it in the morning as you go about doing your morning rituals. Sound therapy suggests that music can shift our brain activity, leaving us feeling relaxed, inspired, and motivated. Research also supports what we already know—that music does benefit our physical and mental health in many ways. It can also reduce anxiety, depression, and stress while improving neurological brain function. Turn on your favorite tunes in the morning to motivate and focus on accomplishing things for the day ahead (Northshore, 2020).

Reading. The question, however, is whether it's better to read in the morning or at night. According to world statistics, it's best to read in the morning. Researchers say that the reason people, mainly adults, do this is to "wake up" and "stimulate" their minds. So grab a book and stimulate your mind before your day begins. It doesn't have to be heavy reading. It could be the news if it means you are saving time later in the day to catch up, or it could be a light-hearted, inspiring book. Just read a couple of pages. If you're trying to lose weight, you can read something motivational for weight loss. Reading at least a page or two may be enough to give you an insightful boost (Aplus, 2022).

LEARNING-BASED ACTION

Creating Your Morning Plan

Now that we have a general idea of how our mornings can be purposeful and look like, that will ultimately set us up for success. Our whole day will begin positively moving in the right direction when you take care of yourself first thing in the morning.

It is dedicated to ensuring that you have created a morning routine that is genuinely purposeful, inspiring, and refreshingly structured to get the day started in the right direction, which is beneficial for your overall well-being.

Step 1

Grab your pen and journal, or open your Master Plan for Life document on your PC or Laptop and go to Chapter 7. If you have not downloaded your digital copy, click or copy and paste the link or go to **https:// go.f4ury.com/knowing-what-you-think-about-is-where-you-will-go** to create your more purposeful morning routine with templated examples so you will not have to start from scratch.

Step 2

Open a new section titled "Morning List." This is where you create your own list of morning activities that you wish to incorporate into your life.

Step 3

Now write down all your favorite activities to explore in a new morning routine, like yoga, meditation, drinking water upon waking, 20-minute cardio work-out, etc.

Step 4

Allocate a time slot for each morning ritual and aim to stick to it.

Step 5

Commit to doing this for 66 days straight without a break in between to rewire your brain to work with you to stick with the new habits.

————————————

After you have completed this exercise, you are ready to move on to the next phase of goal setting. In Chapter 8, we will design your every day. You will get into the habit of taking a step-by-step approach to rewire your neurological connections in the brain to naturally adapt and accept the changes you are about to undertake to change your life.

8

DESIGN YOUR EVERY DAY

> *Live in the present, launch yourself on every wave, and find eternity in each moment.*
>
> — HENRY DAVID THOREAU

STICKING TO THE PLAN

Once you have set your ultimate goal and improved your understanding of your current belief system and how it may be either supporting or sabotaging you, you may be asking yourself, "What next?" You also have some new ideas to transform the manner in which you begin your day. So, the next thing on your list is to examine how you set out to accomplish your tasks every day.

This chapter will provide more insight into how to plan and manage your everyday activities. Planning our daily activities allows us to prioritize what is truly important to us while eliminating things that are mere distractions. So now that we have a good, clear understanding of what you would love to achieve in the short, medium, and long term, our next task is to prioritize activities that are related to achieving those goals.

Becoming purposeful is about ensuring congruence with everything that is meaningful and relevant in our lives. The magic of taking small steps toward success should not be underestimated. This is why staying on track with your short-term goals while holding the long-term vision in your mind's eye remains your priority every day. This is how we plan to succeed when we make every day count!

Make the plan a daily habit. Just as you have committed to kick-starting your day with purposeful mornings, the rest of your day's activities should be aimed at reinforcing this approach with meaningful tasks. Whatever is congruent with your goals—those activities are your high-priority activities to give much energy to. You would need to set deadlines for each task that you wish to accomplish in a month and break them down further into weekly and daily activities, just as you did previously with your short-, medium-, and long-term goals.

Part of the process of designing your every day to be meaningful from the moment of waking up until going to bed must include the elimination of negative habits. These are the habits that are definitely a waste of your precious time and may also be damaging to your health. Choose good, healthy habits to replace the ones that are not adding value to your life and towards the achievement of your goals. For example, if you need to spend less time socializing after work to achieve your short-term goal of studying a new course, then do precisely that. Reprioritize, re-organize, and replenish your every day with new powerful, inspiring habits.

CREATE A 66-DAY HABIT YOU WILL COMMIT

As mentioned earlier, you need at least 66 days of new habits to reprogram your mind into accepting them and making them part of a routine that is more supportive and less self-sabotaging. Give yourself 66 days to effectively repeat your new habit so that it will stick and train the brain and mind to accept new, healthier choices. If you can make it through the initial conditioning phase, it becomes much easier to sustain in the long term.

DESIGN YOUR EVERY DAY IN JUST FIVE STEPS

Here are some simple yet inspiring ways to make new choices when designing your day:

Think like a kid (Develop Curiosity). Be excited like a kid who is just discovering new things for the first time. You are also most likely making new, exciting discoveries about yourself in the process of setting goals and eliminating limiting beliefs. It is therefore expected that you will be feeling a renewed sense of curiosity. Go with it, and decide to commit to exploring your curiosities about all things of significant interest in prioritizing them into daily activities.

Try things out (Build them). Take a leap of faith and simply engage fully in the new activities that you've set out to do each day. Suppose you've been thinking about attending a yoga class but kept postponing it because your mind and limiting thoughts dictated otherwise; change that by giving yourself permission to try new things to replace the old habits. Remember, nothing changes if you keep doing the same things but expect different results.

How reframing the problem is important. Choose to reframe any problems or challenges that come up for you as you progress on your new journey. Be consistently mindful of the labels that you attach to these problems, and also take cognizance of how you approach these problems and challenges. See things on the way instead of in the way, and soon you will be overcoming these little setbacks brilliantly and confidently.

It is just a process (Learning from the good and the bad experience). Treat every encounter as a unique opportunity to learn and grow from. However, also accept that in the process, some learning experiences may be more painful than others. Developing a simple awareness about what you are facing each day, and doing your best to overcome these with an acceptance that there will be some pain, will keep you centered on what is important to you. You need to be unwavering and relentless in the pursuit of your goals, with a mind-frame that is determined to learn from and grow from all experiences and encounters.

Seek guidance. Don't be afraid of seeking advice and assistance when required to help you overcome setbacks better or learn the application of new skills. Explore ways that you can benefit from the knowledge of others with similar interests. Stand on the shoulders of giants as you make your way toward the attainment of your goals. Have fun, learn, and embrace new experiences.

BREAK THE PLAN INTO SMALLER DAILY THINGS TO DO

The best advice that mindfulness experts offer is to simply take life one day at a time. Aim to be fully present and actively involved in all areas of your life and all of your tasks each and every day. You will be very thankful at the end of it, and your mind will be receiving the training it needs to avoid shifting to aimless thoughts that will undoubtedly distract you from your tasks once you give them attention.

Having a vision remains relevant to living your best life. Taking small steps and thinking big is a magic formula for success. Those small steps that you take each and every day to arrive at the destination of your goals must be relevant and purposeful, and they must build enough momentum to inspire you throughout the journey of goal attainment. The little things count, so don't undervalue the small steps that are required of you each and every day to get to your desired achievement.

If you've committed to this, read for half an hour to improve your leadership skills, and by all means, give every action your best shot! Remember that the magic of your new journey lies in your ability to consistently take small steps each and every day. Consistency remains vital, and living life fully, one day at a time, will bring more feelings of satisfaction to your life.

RELOOKING AT YOUR UNIQUE GOAL PLAN

Reevaluating your goals is essential when taking action toward their realization. The journey of goal setting will open you up to new possibilities—this means that just as the universe keeps expanding, so will your imagination and creativity. Tweaking your goals makes sense when you are constantly building momentum toward the realization of your life's mission. One idea can lead to a dozen more when you are engaged in daily tasks to accomplish your goals. For instance, while writing your first book (if that was a goal), you may receive flashes of insight and inspiration to write several more books to create an entire series that are relevant to your ongoing journey.

Avoid taking a monolithic approach to your action plan. Allow for flexibility, and keep your heart open to flashes of inspiration as you progress. We must be alert to how, through the power of the subconscious mind, we can continuously attract synchronicity into our lives. Attention goes where energy flows! As you progress towards the attainment of your goals and gain more confidence, coincidences will no longer seem like a chance of fate but rather like a purposeful message from the Universe that your efforts keep you experiencing meaningful encounters each day. This is what synchronicity is all about, attracting the right people, situations, opportunities, and outcomes to your life.

As your dreams, desires, and gifts evolve, so will your goals. Whenever you are struck with new inspiration, insights, and inspiring revelations, re-evaluating your goals will make perfect sense. It will also inspire you to consistently refresh your goals to keep them relevant to your ongoing journey. In this way, you will also achieve consistent clarity and know instinctively, based on your ongoing experience, what is working and what isn't.

Don't be regretful for feeling intuitively guided to strike out goals that may no longer seem relevant. It is part of the creative process to change certain goals, set new ones, or even change direction altogether when you receive new insight, flashes of inspiration, and experiential wisdom. This is why it is essential to look at your daily things-to-do list, in the evenings. In this way, you will be prepared the next day to tackle your high-priority tasks, which may be shifting constantly based on your progress.

RINSE AND REPEAT FOR CONTINUED SUCCESS

Our habits manage our lives, literally. Research shows that about half of our daily actions are driven by repetition. This is perhaps why behavioral scientists and psychologists have spent so much time writing about establishing and keeping positive habits. Regular sleep and exercise, a healthy diet, a more organized schedule, and mindfulness are all practices that—if done regularly—can enhance our work, relationships, and mental health.

Have a clear intention on why you want to accomplish this goal and the desired outcome. This is how you can stick to the schedule or plan you have created for yourself. The why and intended effect of repetitive action will remind you of why you want to achieve your goal, and it will become much easier to accomplish.

There is no exact science because everyone is different based on their beliefs, cognitive learning ability, and the values that create who they are. But if the desired outcome is strong enough to inspire change, only through daily action can you recreate your life as desired. Only repetitive action reinforces your desire to achieve your goal. This is the only method, and honestly, there are no shortcuts. You have to put in the work. And through time, your repetitive actions will be formed into habits that help you achieve your desired goal.

As a reminder, reviewing your daily schedule in the evening is essential and will be subconsciously embedded in your mind when you sleep. Then, when you wake up, you will know exactly what you need to accomplish for the day. Also, this gives you time to reflect on the day's activities without judging what went right and wrong and build upon or improve it with your new daily evening routine. Then rinse, repeat, and modify your plan if needed as you develop your new life into a routine.

LEARNING-BASED ACTION

Identifying Habits That No Longer Serve You

These are the habits you will identify to make the changes needed to create improved practices in your life to achieve success within your ultimate goal plan. When you continuously practice, your brain will accept these changes naturally, becoming autonomic, just like how you naturally breathe and will be a part of your new life journey. You will bring back to focus the long-term vision of the future you want to create.

Step 1

Grab your pen and journal, or open your Master Plan for Life document on your PC or Laptop and go to Chapter 8. If you have not downloaded your digital copy, click or copy and paste the link or go to **https://go.f4ury.com/knowing-what-you-think-about-is-where-you-will-go** to be able to clearly identify what habits are not serving you and how to develop new habits of success.

Step 2

Pull out your Morning List, and re-evaluate the changes you needed to make to your mornings for them to be more meaningful, energizing, and relevant.

Step 3

Now, identify the habits that you would need to change to make more time to occupy yourself with tasks that are aligned with your goals.

For example: If you've identified the need to engage in more physical activity in the evenings to support your health goals, you would need to strike that item off the list by having a beer in the afternoons with your colleagues.

Step 4

Once you've identified and taken stock of all your daily habits that may be standing in the way of your success, replace them with relevant new habits, and write down how each of these new habits will benefit the attainment of your goals in the long term.

Step 5

Finally, create a new daily routine for your next day that incorporates relevant, high-priority tasks matched with new habits that are supportive of your new goals.

Once you've developed new habits of success to rid yourself of living a life of mediocrity to living a life by your design, we can now move on to the next phase of goal setting. In Chapter 9, we will highlight the importance of feeling a strong desire to achieve your goals and dreams. Without a strong desire for your goals and dreams, they will remain only as a memory trapped inside your subconscious mind collecting dust. Desire plus action is the formula for success motivating you to get to your destination.

9

UNDERSTANDING THE POWER OF DESIRE

> *The future belongs to those who believe in the beauty of their dreams.*
>
> — ELEANOR ROOSEVELT

The more desire you have, the easier it will be to accomplish anything in no time. Desire is the spark of all dreams. When we know and feel deeply that we should follow a specific path in life, and if we are willing to do whatever it takes to achieve our goals, our chances of success improve significantly. This proved to be true for me throughout my career in the military. I was determined to build a wonderful career for myself, and I grabbed all opportunities that came my way with both hands. My appetite for learning, growing and realizing my greatest potential as a leader heightened with each new opportunity that presented itself to me. Of course, life wasn't always peachy, but it sure became a lot more meaningful, purposeful, and fulfilling for me.

Everyone has the free will to choose their desired outcome in life—this is what it means to be limitless! Everyone has the potential to live out their dreams, desires, and aspirations. Desire is what fuels us and propels us into action. To be open and to feel limitless, we must first embrace our desire to succeed. When we do this, we will also be willing to embrace both opportunities and challenges and regard them as stepping-stones to our success. We were not born to be unlimited.

It does not matter what your background is, where you were born, or how you were raised. First, it starts with knowing who you are and where you want to be in the future. It does not have to do with your environment or the social networks you belong to, either. Everyone has free will to choose their desired outcome in life.

Yes, some people who were born into rough situations or environments did not choose this for themselves. That is understandable. But we have thousands of thoughts going through our minds every day; some are good, and some are not. Somewhere in your mind, you have probably heard the little voice in your head telling you that your situation can be better.

That is why, if you have had these types of thoughts going through your mind, you know instinctively that the power of choice is also simply a thought away from turning your dreams into a reality that you will be proud of. You do have the power within you to turn your "if only" into real possibilities. You don't need to be born on the right side of the tracks to make your dreams a reality. You just need to stick with your plan, be relentless, and stay on track with what is most important to you. Allow desire to fuel you into inspired action.

STAYING ON TRACK

Every emotion we feel as soon as we wake up and throughout the day is an integral part of how the day will feel for us. Staying on track is more than just exercising willpower. Making a conscious effort to stick to your plan of action daily, fueled by a strong desire and determination, is what will give you the results you need to achieve for your life, to shape up according to your vision. Harnessing that power from within to reach the summit of your success, also includes following a structured, well-managed approach to your personal and professional development.

As we've already learned from earlier chapters, our emotions can also sabotage our success. This is why it is important to deliberately create positive emotions and reinforce our goals and action plans. When you are facing decisions that need to be made that will shape the outcome of your future, base those decisions on what is most important to you, not on negative emotions, but on a controlled perspective to achieve results.

For example, if you're facing a rude and angry customer and feel that you're being minimized unnecessarily, think of your long-term vision and ask your-self if it would be worth it to make the situation worse or better. You won't need to waste more energy argu-ing; instead, you can be inspired to achieve a more favorable outcome based on your desire to take your business to new heights of success. Simply remember what you are going after and why it is important to you whenever you reflect on your choices at any given moment in time. This will keep you solidly on track, focused, and inspired to solve problems based on your long-term interests.

Use Your Emotions to Guide You Forward

When we are excited, engaged, enthused, and dreaming about new possibilities, we are most likely to stay on track with what is most important to us! These positive emotions need to be reinforced when-ever you are reflecting on your goals—in a meditative state, by using the power of visualization to tap into those emotions, you will also be powerfully rewiring your subconscious mind to react positively towards your goal achievements.

Therefore, when going through your goals daily, make sure that your desire is congruent with your goals and that your determination is intact. Visualize the quality of life and how it is constantly changing to reflect your core values, beliefs, and desires. Your life will start changing remarkably once you consistently internalize your desire to accomplish your goals. Beliefs fueled by desire and acted upon by inspired decisions, will leave a remarkable trail of positive outcomes in your life, ones that you can be proud of.

If you are not feeling excited, enthused, and even hypnotized by the possibilities that lie ahead when considering your plans for the future, then you are most likely completely off track. This is why human behavior experts reinforce the idea that we must simply do what we love. Motivation is strongest when positive emotions are attached to our activities.

Always Highlight Your Goal in the Morning

The importance of constantly waking up with your goal in mind cannot be reiterated enough. When we start our day, we must remind ourselves of what is important, sacred, and relevant to us. When we do this, we also subconsciously eliminate things that are low priorities.

Use the first 20 minutes of your morning after waking up to reflect quietly on your goals and priorities. Set positive thoughts in motion, and feel what you are going after inside your body. Make it real, tangible, and achievable in your mind. When you believe it and feel it, you are bringing it to life for your subconscious mind to fully embrace. This is how we train our minds to engage positively with our vision, and goals when they have just woken up.

Listen to Your Intuition to Avoid Over-Thinking

The brain will not make you happy; it is only there and designed only for the primary purpose of survival and as a protection mechanism. The only way to get the mind to work for you, not against you, is to train it.

You did the hard part; you have become aware of your belief system and understand what core values are essential to you, and you now have a plan for your goals and daily tasks on hand. This is one of the methods for training the mind to work with you because you have started every day with your goal in mind.

Sometimes, when making big decisions, it is best to listen to your inner self, quiet the mind, and listen to what you are trying to tell yourself. Then look at how it makes you feel. At times, you already know what you need to do; your intuition tells you to go all in. Think of your intuition as your inner *Master* who is always ready to provide you with the necessary counsel to ensure that you are continuously aligned with your core values and are not doing anything that doesn't feel right.

Intuition may also be guided by knowledge. So, if you are in any doubt about your decisions, gather more knowledge and sit with your intuition as it feels its way through the information coming through from your conscious mind to ascertain whether a decision will be in your best and highest interest. If this advice might sound strange to you, then fear not, because it simply means that exploring and trusting your inner master based on your desire to succeed might be new to you.

There are plenty of entrepreneurs and top-achieving individuals in the world today who swear by the promptings of their intuition. Oprah Winfrey is one such entrepreneur who always follows her intuition in all situations.

"I've trusted the still, small voice of intuition my entire life. And the only time I've made mistakes is when I didn't listen. It's really more of a feeling than a voice—a whispery sensation that pulsates just beneath the surface of your being. All animals have it. We're the only creatures that deny and ignore it." (para. 1–2)

You may have already witnessed your intuition at work but could not put a label on it. So let me help you out here. It is a gut feeling that washes over us at times, a deep knowing that something feels right or off. It is simply an instinctual response that is not linked directly to your subconscious mind. It's almost like an animal instinct that can sense when something feels right for you or not. I doubt there is a single person alive who hasn't wished that they had followed their intuition more than they have and who can vouch for the many regrets in life they've experienced based on their decisions not to follow their intuition.

Here's a quick rule of thumb that you can implement in your life to help you follow your intuition more. Only by making quick decisions can you fully commit to what is important to you right out of the gate without letting doubt and worry slowly kill your decision over time. When making a choice, you can use a 3- to 5-second rule to decide so that your thinking brain will not sabotage you and you can quickly move forward with executing your plan. This will reduce your procrastination mind from making you doubt yourself and not complete the task at hand. Then you will be one step closer to achieving your ultimate goal.

LEARNING-BASED ACTION

Rating Your Inner Desire to Achieve Your Goals

The way to stay on track is to use your emotions of desire to remain vigilant and diligently highlight your goals daily. Do not allow your emotions to overtake you and overthink things; use the emotions of your intuition to guide you forward.

You will not go wrong when you quiet your mind to understand what you are trying to tell yourself, and you will know what to do next. Let's get started below to rate your inner desire to achieve your goals.

Step 1

Grab your pen and journal, or open your Master Plan for Life document on your PC or Laptop and go to Chapter 9. If you have not downloaded your digital copy, click or copy and paste the link or go to **https://go.f4ury.com/knowing-what-you-think-about-is-where-you-will-go** to enable yourself to go deeper within yourself to use the power of emotional desire to propel you forward to achieving your goals.

Step 2

Consult your list of goals for each area of your life that you've highlighted, as well as your long, medium, and short-term goals.

Step 3

Rate how strong your desire is for the attainment of each goal, and also highlight how you would feel if you did not give it your best shot!

Step 4

Regard how you would feel if you decided now to simply disregard your Master Plan for Life, and continue living your life as you are now.

If you are satisfied that your desire to succeed is strong—much stronger than remaining stuck where you are now in life—then you are, without a doubt, ready and determined to turn your dreams into reality.

Step 5

Go through the lists one more time and ask yourself:

What does your intuition feel like when looking over your goals? Does it feel right for you, or are you feeling any sense of discomfort in any areas of your life?

If you are feeling any discomfort, then go deeper and question exactly what is making you uncomfortable. Just note it down to seek clarity from within on the adjustments that you would need to make.

You made it to the final chapter, where we will bring together your *7-Way Action Plan For Your Success!* Now is the time to ingrain what you have learned, understanding how beliefs, values, and thoughts can affect the daily decision-making process that can hold us back from achieving success.

When understanding how the brain works, the conscious and subconscious mind can either work for us or against us. When learning something new, you can focus on what is valuable to your life and create new habits, making new neurological connections in your brain to accept the life you want—making life much easier and more manageable.

10

BRINGING IT ALL TOGETHER— YOUR 7-WAY ACTION PLAN TO ACHIEVE YOUR SUCCESS

> *It's the possibility of making a dream come true that makes life interesting.*
>
> — PAULO COELHO

SEVEN POWERFUL STEPS TO ACHIEVE SUCCESS

I n this chapter, you will put it all together, the 7-Way Action Plan For Success. This is where the magic happens, and this is where you will begin to shift your awareness to a new world of possibilities. You can again start believing in your dreams, knowing that you can create them to become your new reality.

You have read and worked through this book's contents to become aware that you can reprogram your subconscious mind and put more energy behind your *7-Way Action Plan For Your Success*. If there are any chapters or steps you may have skipped, please complete all the Learning-Based Actions at the end of each chapter. If you have finished them all, then pat yourself on the back for taking inspired action to bring it all together for you—to activate the essential changes you want to implement in your life.

Since commencing your inspiring work in your Master Plan for Life Journal, in Chapter 1, you have discovered and noticed some remarkable changes in your thinking. You have now activated the executive center of your brain to work for you to become consciously aware of where you want your life to go.

This is where you have probably been thinking of ways to implement your plan, and that's super!

You have also been thinking about your belief system and the limiting beliefs that may still be grabbing hold of your life. This is how you have started transforming your brain's chemistry and mindset. Just by reading and following through with the exercises, you will soon be amazed at the profound changes taking place in your life as you put your shoulder to the wheel to get things going in a matter of days!

You finished drafting your long, medium, and short-term goals and are now working through the various exercises. This has allowed you to achieve absolute clarity, focus, and inspiration in all areas of your life where you want change to happen. This enabled you to push yourself to examine your habits and contemplate the value of replacing them with new, inspiring ones that will bring you closer to achieving your goals. We have already done a lot together to bring you closer to living your most authentic and inspiring life —the life you were born to live.

After working through all the exercises, you will most definitely begin to feel good about your future prospects. You have brought certainty into your life that brings about hope and confidence, and you can start walking with a bounce in your steps once again, knowing that what we think about is where we will go! Before we dive in completely to recap before topping off the 7-Way Action Plan For Your Success, there are some concepts that I would love to introduce to you. These are important to reflect upon, as they will help you move your mind toward positively engaging in achieving your greatest potential.

HOW TO REACH FULL POTENTIAL
IDENTIFYING SELF-ACTUALIZATION

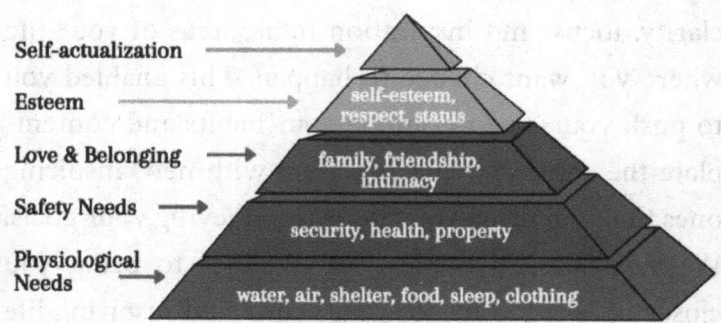

Maslow's Hierarchy of Needs

Self-actualization

Esteem → self-esteem, respect, status

Love & Belonging → family, friendship, intimacy

Safety Needs → security, health, property

Physiological Needs → water, air, shelter, food, sleep, clothing

It was Abraham Maslow, a prominent psychologist, who introduced the concept of self-actualization in 1943 in his Theory of Motivation. In this publication, he identified critical human needs in a pyramid depicting the lowest to the highest human needs. This theory stipulates that human beings are motivated to progress through the various levels of need to reach the highest point of what he called self-actualization.

Maslow believed that people have an inherent need to actualize their fullest potential and that this state of self-actualization varies from person to person. He also believed that humans must first climb the levels of needs that he identified in his pyramid of needs. The lowest level starts with our need for food; it then moves on to other needs such as safety, love, and self-esteem. The top level of the pyramid is self-actualization.

Maslow's theory has been taught and used across the world in all studies of human behavior to explain what is widely accepted as truth about our need to feel a sense of purpose and a desire to fulfill that inherent desire to reach one's fullest potential.

This pyramid can also help you track your progress as you move beyond the first levels of need satisfaction. It's important to keep this in mind because human nature is such that reaching self-actualization all at once would become increasingly challenging. Acknowledge that it is the journey of getting to the top of the pyramid that really matters, who you become in the process, and how you define success along your entire journey forward (Cherry, 2022).

Know About Positive Psychology

From a psychological perspective, goals play a very decisive role in how we think about ourselves, life in general, and others. We positively validate our authenticity when we have goals and congruently take action toward their attainment. Positive psychology is about taking steps towards achieving our goals that will predictably lead to a higher feeling of self-confidence, self-respect, self-love, and self-esteem. The underlying value of incorporating positive psychology into our lives centers around finding meaning by setting goals, and achieving those goals is the only way to feel fulfilled about life.

Tony Robbins is a world-famous motivational speaker. He is known for helping millions of people across the globe embrace this positive psychology in their lives. "Setting goals is the first step from turning the invisible to visible" (BA, 2010, para.17). Positive psychology, therefore, involves understanding what drives us and training our minds to consistently move towards self-actualization. When we train our minds, focus on what we want, and work towards fulfilling those goals, positive psychology is the process of constantly reinforcing thoughts and acting to reach self-actualization. Creating Your Potential

When we know how to use positive psychology in our favor to boost our thoughts and train ourselves through discipline and hard work, we can achieve our greatest potential to shift gears from living a life of mediocrity to fulfilling one of the great possibilities. Below you will read other areas to contemplate and reflect upon to ensure that positive psychology further guarantees success in living the life you want to create. The following are mental processes you can embrace daily to ensure that what you think about brings you to your final destination and even beyond your wildest expectations! You will begin to be and feel limitless as you incorporate the positive psychological approach to fine-tune your thoughts, beliefs, habits, and behaviors to the life you want to live.

Growth Mindset vs. Fixed Mindset

Commit to adopting a growth mindset instead of being fixed and rigid in your thinking processes. A growth mindset embraces change, is open to learning new skills constantly, and creatively engages in all situations to ensure personal and professional growth.

You will be more aware of your surroundings, be open to new possibilities and opportunities, and be willing to change your current situation. On the other hand, a fixed mindset can have a very limited perspective on embracing change. It is rigidly fixated on old beliefs, habits, and behaviors that are hardwired to accept mediocrity easily and will, therefore, not be open to adapting quickly to new situations or being aware of new opportunities or possibilities. When facing challenges that deserve our attention, if we want to succeed in any environment, we need to develop a growth mindset because this is the only way to learn and change where we want our life to go to achieve success.

Reflect and Take Action

Be willing to consistently reflect on your life and goals, streamline them, and assess your course of action. This also means caving into fear of the unknown when something appears to not be working out in your favor. Remember that when anything does not meet your expectations, it is simply a sign for you to reflect on the "why" and to assess a new way forward. It does not mean giving up on your dreams and goals entirely, but simply having the courage and desire to achieve success in the face of challenges with a realistic attitude and willingness to win and adapt to be more flexible in one's plans. And by all means, be patient. It is not a race to reach your final destination, but a marathon to embrace the journey that will safely get you to your desired end goal.

Focus on the Big Picture

If you stick solidly to your routine, you will revisit your long, medium, and short-term goals daily. When things do not go as planned, always remember that the magic I keep referring to is to focus on the big picture; your vision is how you will get what you want out of life. The short-, medium-, and long-term accomplishments you aim for in your life will be the results for which you aim.

Merely going about your daily tasks monotonously and not focusing on your goals can sometimes lead to frustration. This happens when we lose sight of the big picture, not appreciating how every step toward realizing our goals counts in our favor. There are no shortcuts. You have to find like-minded, inspirational people or groups to belong to or books to read that align with you and your vision of the future. This is how you regain control of your life when you focus on your long-term vision for the future.

Recharge When Needed

Finally, ensure your daily self-care routine does not fall by the wayside when your schedule intensifies. Make the time to recharge when this happens, especially if you neglect your self-care routine every now and then. It is vital to consistently care for our body and mind to nurture positive thoughts, actions, and physical vitality.

Now I have provided a road map or blueprint that you can utilize to create the new life that you want to create. You can follow through on the vital concepts that will further remind you of the "big why" to achieve your goals. It is time to put everything together in an easy "7-Way Action Plan For Your Success," which you've been creating throughout this book. This is where you will need to constantly rinse and repeat the process to reinforce continued success and see shifts in your life happen right before your eyes.

Grab your pen and journal or open the document on your PC or Laptop. Go to Chapter 10 in your document. Or if you still need to download your digital copy, click or copy and paste the link or go to **https:// go.f4ury.com/knowing-what-you-think-about-is- where-you-will-go.**

You made it this far, and now is the time to commit to getting started and get your free digital copy of your *Master Plan for Life Journal* to change your life. If you have been using the provided journal and finishing each Learning-Based Acton in this book, then pat yourself on the back. Now you are ready to make a contractual agreement with yourself with your *7-Way Action Plan For Your Success.*

ACTION 1: REVIEW AND IDENTIFY YOUR BELIEF SYSTEMS AND HOW THEY MAY IMPACT YOUR GOAL

We began our journey in Chapters 1 and 2, where we identified and learned how our core beliefs had been implanted into our minds through daily interactions that were perceived to be accurate. We also determined our limiting beliefs in this part of the journey. Our beliefs that are limiting come across as being negative and lead us to take on a narrower approach to life, especially with respect to setting and reaching our goals.

Therefore, we set out how to identify, eliminate, and replace them with positive, inspiring beliefs aimed at unlocking your true potential. Review what you've written in your Master Plan for Life Journal, where you've identified your limiting beliefs, and reflect on how they may still be holding you back. Focus on moving forward by letting go of these limiting beliefs that keep you stuck in frustration, and self-sabotaging ways. This will assist you in further identifying what you may need to do to create new beliefs that will energize you to achieve your goals.

ACTION 2: THE WAY YOU THINK AND HOW IT IMPACTS GOAL ATTAINMENT

We must remind ourselves to be aware of what we think about and what we persistently give energy to. Remember that the subconscious mind records every experience through the neurological connections in our brain. The subconscious mind is a powerful part of your brain and prioritizes every thought, desire, feeling, and need. Therefore, Chapter 3 entails that we take cognizance of why we need to train our brains to work for us instead of against us. We must make a conscious effort to shift our thoughts from negative to positive. You've now learned how to unlock negativity from your past and use those lessons as a learning tool to positively change how you relate to past events. This is how we rewire those neurological connections to create better outcomes.

You also closely explored how you can train your subconscious mind to create deliberate new experiences that will support the development of new ideas and goals. You discovered how to change your beliefs into more positive ones that will take you closer to realizing your goals and achieving joy and happiness in your journey. Changing your mind is how you change your life, so review what you wrote and what you are willing to do to change your mind.

ACTION 3: DEVELOP THE PLAN

You developed your ultimate goal plan because, without a map, you cannot go anywhere, which picks up the pace in Chapters 4, 5, and 6. Chapters 4 and 5 provided clarity on the path forward to constantly develop and improve yourself, personally and professionally, and also to look at what you value most in life for the development of your goals. You learned how to create meaningful strategies based entirely on the essential core values you've identified as relevant for every area of your life in your Master Plan for Life Journal.

In Chapter 6, you developed your initial draft of your long-, medium-, and short-term goals. Here, you used everything you learned from all the previous chapters to get you to take inspired new actions that are relevant to your goals. You achieved a great amount of clarity in every area of your life to accomplish things that are most meaningful to you. Now it is time to put your ultimate goal plan into deliberate action.

ACTION 4: IMPLEMENT THE PLAN

For your ultimate goal plan to work for you, the prioritization of your day starts upon waking up (Chapter 7). This will help you improve your mood and energy flow for the rest of the day. You learned the importance of creating structure in your life and embraced new ideas to ensure that your mornings are purposeful, inspiring, and aligned with activities that will boost your inspiration. The focus of Chapter 7 is to highlight the importance of taking care of yourself first thing in the morning to accomplish your day's goals.

ACTION 5: ALIGNMENT WITH CORE VALUES TO RE-EVALUATE THE PLAN

Our focus shifted from creating purposeful mornings to designing your every day in Chapter 8. From the moment you wake up to the moment you go to sleep, your day must be meaningfully planned. Be very detailed at first, and then see what you have been doing in a day or a week. Then you will better understand what things you need to remove or modify in your schedule or life.

Once you understand what one week may look like, plan on doing your one task for 30 days to reach your goal. If you think you can do more daily tasks, add them to your daily and weekly schedule. Set up milestones for when you need to achieve a specific goal and include days to reward yourself. Within your 30-day evaluation of your daily and weekly tasks, review your values to see if they align with your goals and vision for the future. And what you may need to do internally to modify your thinking into your ultimate goal plan.

ACTION 6: STICKING TO THE PLAN

In Chapter 9, we discovered how important it is to stick to your 30-day mission of developing new and improved habits. It takes 66 days (Chapter 3) for your brain to adapt to recent changes for your new neurological connections in the brain to get implanted long-term to form a new habit. We learned how important it is to use your emotions to boost your desire and visualize your goals daily, listening to your little voice, intuition, or gut instinct when making important decisions. Remember the three to five-second rule to make decisions quickly; this will help with procrastination.

ACTION 7: STAYING ON TRACK WITH THE PLAN

Finally, commit to staying on track with your plan. Highlight your focal points in the evening before the start of your new day. When you are focused on your priorities for the day, you will be moving forward all the time, toward the realization of your goals. Seek support from your inner circle to keep you on track. It does make a difference to have support, encouragement, and someone you can talk to about your ongoing journey.

Trust your intuition when reflecting on your plan of action, and be willing to make adjustments. Be prepared for unexpected setbacks, and continuously re-plan and re-evaluate everything you have learned about your journey and yourself. Modify your goals when necessary, if something is not working or feeling right for you. Also, don't forget to be kind to yourself and permit yourself to take a break to recharge yourself.

Once you have reevaluated your current situation, will you quit, or will you find alternatives to make your goals more attainable? Remember that everything we do really depends on us to make it happen for ourselves. Only you can take responsibility for what matters most to you in your life; no one else will! So now you know how to create your own Master Plan for Life. Taking inspired action with consistent perseverance will surely get you to your destination.

CONCLUSION

We set out on an inspiring journey together; when you bought this book, I hope you reached a new level of awareness that we can change our desired destiny in life at any given moment. I am confident that you followed through on this journey, exploring a renewed sense of purpose and meaning in your life. Ultimately, I hope this book has changed your life the same way that the *Silva Method* changed mine when it miraculously fell on my lap in 1999. I hope you were encouraged by the topics that we covered quite extensively in this book—our beliefs, our values, and how the mind works based on neuroscientific discoveries allow us to create change from within.

There are no coincidences in life. Our paths were meant to cross. We were destined to take this amazing journey together. You've now discovered something truly valuable that will continuously impact your life. You see, it really boils down to what we think about, which determines where we will end up going in life. As I highlighted throughout the book, our brain is the miracle center waiting for us to tap into its potential to serve us for our greatest development and highest purpose in life. How you think and feel about who you are will ultimately measure up against what manifests in your daily life. Knowing this now places the power in your hands to dictate your life's destiny.

When you genuinely focus on this book's contents, your life will never be the same again. Understanding how the mind works is a transformative experience. Already it must have registered in your thoughts just how we need to be accountable to ourselves for the quality of the lives we want to create. Even if you end up just reading or listening to this book without doing the exercises in your first read, the chances of shifting your perception within yourself are still quite great. Sometimes all it takes are a few inspiring words to create change from within.

However, if you have completed all the exercises honestly and earnestly, your chances of shifting your life have already quadrupled. When you truly understand and learn how our thoughts and actions are connected to our subconscious mind, you will understand how to harness the power of change from within to reach your goals. When you create your ultimate goal plan, this is how you are directing your subconscious mind to support your vision for the future, unhindered by past wounds or limiting beliefs.

The past has already happened, and you cannot change it. Learning from your past beliefs and values and how they held you back opens up your consciousness to new ways of creating change in your life. As you've learned, every step forward counts, no matter how big or small. But more than just knowing this, you must take action from the moment your feet hit the ground in the morning. Creating intense, purposeful outcomes daily is when YOU have taken power over your life and decided that you will no longer be a victim of circumstances, but a master of destiny. You now have a powerful 7-Way Action Plan For Your Success and are ready to create massive change, one day at a time.

Feel free to share this wisdom of knowledge, with others and help them to also become unstuck from mediocrity. I wrote this book, *Knowing What You Think About Is Where You Will Go*, to share knowledge with you through my observations of my personal and professional life experiences—to change your life—and to leave you feeling accountable, empowered, and inspired to pass on this knowledge to others. This is how I successfully created my military life to impact the many military service members and local nationals I worked alongside in the U.S. and in different countries I have been stationed.

I have had the privilege of leading and inspiring them to transform their lives from within. As I move forward with my civilian life, I wish to be of service to you so you can share the knowledge you've discovered here with your family, friends, peers, and your inner circles. You can help others see a different perspective on how they can truly live inspiring lives.

Please leave a book review from the bookseller you purchased the book from, about what you have discovered and learned from this book. I am sure many more people will be encouraged by your thoughts and insights into what you have learned and also get inspired. Also, do visit me on my website, F4URY.com. I would love to hear from you and your story. Here you will also find the necessary resources in one place to discover new ways of finding meaning in life. You will find out more about other topics that I am passionate about, like health, love, wealth, and happiness to help improve people's lives.

I wish you much success in your future endeavors. My humblest and greatest gratitude to you for reading or listening to my book—I know that great things await you, and I am excited about what you plan to change in your life.

A Free Gift to Our Readers: Download Your Master Plan For Life Journal

The Journal references a chapter-by-chapter guide with actions, steps, and strategies that follows the book to save a copy on your PC or Laptop. This will assist you in putting your Master Plan for Life in motion faster for continued success and tracking your progress so you will not have to start from scratch.

Scan QR Code to Get Access Or Visit the Link Below

https://go.f4ury.com/knowing-what-you-think-about-is-where-you-will-go

When you download your Journal, you will get a book compilation email series to assist you in staying motivated and on track throughout your journey together.

For your success!

REFERENCES

Antonio, S. (2016). *Refusing negative thoughts from entering your mind* [Video]. YouTube. www.youtube.com/watch?v=82oOH POBKA8.

Brown, L. (2020, June 21). *14 things to do in the morning to have a better day.* https://hackspirit.com/a-harvard-psychologist-says-this-is-the-first-thing-you-should-do-when-you-wake-up-in-the-morning/

Cherry, K. (2020). *How cognitive biases influence how you think and act.* Verywell Mind. https://www.verywellmind.com/what-is-a-cognitive-bias-2794963

Cherry, K. (2022, August 14). *How Maslow's Famous Hierarchy of Needs Explains Human Motivation.* Verywell Mind. https://www.verywellmind.com/what-is-maslows-hierarchy-of-needs-4136760

Clear, J. (2018, July 13). *How Long Does It Actually Take to Form a New Habit?* James Clear. https://jamesclear.com/new-habit

Cognitive learning therapy. (n.d.). The Peak Performance Center. https://thepeakperformancecenter.com/educational-learning/learning/theories/cognitive-learning-theory/

Dasgupta, R. (2020, July 20). *Sleep Inertia: Symptoms, Causes, Treatments, and More.* Healthline. https://www.healthline.com/health/sleep/how-to-deal-with-sleep-inertia

Demartini, Dr. J. (n.d.). *Dr. John Demartini.* Huffington Post. https://www.huffpost.com/author/dr-john-demartini

Dietrich, C. (2010). *Decision Making: Factors that Influence Decision Making, Heuristics Used, and Decision Outcomes.* Inquiries Journal. http://www.inquiriesjournal.com/articles/180/decision-making-factors-that-influence-decision-making-heuristics-used-and-decision-outcomes

Dispenza, J. (2015). *You are the placebo: making your mind matter.* Hay House, Inc.

Eight Ways to Develop Metacognitive Skills. (n.d.). InnerDrive. https://blog.innerdrive.co.uk/eight-ways-to-develop-metacognitive-skills

Eleven Reasons Why You Should Do The Things You Love. (n.d.) (2016, March 7). Pick The Brain. https://www.pickthebrain.com/11-reasons-things-love

Ellis, L. (2021, March 14). *What Is Oprah Winfrey's Daily Routine?* Celeb Answers. https://celebanswers.com/what-is-oprah-winfreys-daily-routine

Fleming, Dr. K. (n.d.). *The Executive Brain.* https://www.all-about-psychology.com/the-executive-brain.html

Garone, S. (2018, September 6). *13 Quick Ways to Banish Morning Fatigue.* Healthline. https://www.healthline.com/health/morning-fatigue-remedies#13.-Ultimately

Grind, B. the. (2021, January 14). *Bill Gates: Daily Routine.* Medium. https://medium.com/daily-routines-of-successful-people/bill-gates-daily-routine-fb64df94a175

Haas, T. de. (2011, September 1). *What is a Belief?* About my brain. https://www.aboutmybrain.com/blog/what-is-a-belief

Hall, M. (2010, February 9). *Beliefs #2: The Meta-Levels of Beliefs.* https://www.neurosemantics.com/beliefs-2-the-meta-levels-of-beliefs/

How Do Belief Systems Impact Your Decisions? (2018, October 12). Networks, M. H. O. https://blog.mho.com/how-do-belief-systems-impact-your-decisions

Kendra Cherry. (2019, July 9). *How the Perceptual Process Works With Our Environment.* Verywell Mind. https://www.verywellmind.com/perception-and-the-perceptual-process-2795839

Lynch, M. (2018, August 15). *What is Cognitive Learning?* The Tech

Advocate https://www.thetechedvocate.org/what-is-cognitive-learning/

McDowell, E. (2019, July 14). *20 rags to riches stories that will blow your mind*. Business Insider. https://www.businessinsider.co.za/millionaires-billionaires-who-came-from-nothing-rags-to-riches-stories-2019-7?r=US&IR=T

Modi, J. (2021, August 1). *Plato Meaning of Life*. Good Question. https://goodqn.com/meaning-of-life-plato/

Nine Health Benefits of Music. (2020, December 31). NorthShore University Health System. https://www.northshore.org/healthy-you/9-health-benefits-of-music/

Peterson, A. L. (n.d.). *7 Health Benefits of Sunlight*. Select Health. https://selecthealth.org/blog/2020/07/7-health-benefits-of-sunlight

Rao, SathyanarayanaT. S., Asha, M., Rao, JagannathaK. S., & Vasudevaraju, P. (2009). *The biochemistry of belief*. Indian Journal of Psychiatry. https://doi.org/10.4103/0019-5545.58285

Raw Chemistry. (2020, February 3). *Cortisol stress has 7 really negative effects on the body*. Raw Chemistry. https://rawchemistry.com/blogs/news/cortisol-stress-has-7-really-negative-effects-on-the-body

Reeves, C. (2018, October 6). *Neurons That Fire Together Wire Together*. The Mind is the Map. https://themindisthemap.com/neurons-that-fire-together-wire-together/

Romanell, A. (2020, January 5). *Core Beliefs: The Hammer We Hold in Our Hand*. Psychology Today. https://www.psychologytoday.com/us/blog/the-other-side-relationships/202001/core-beliefs-the-hammer-we-hold-in-our-hand

Seshadri, N. (n.d.). *The power of intuition. Why is it so rare?* Mind And Soul. https://mindandsoul.space/home/2019/4/13/the-power-of-intuition-why-is-it-so-rare

Sharma, A. (2014, January 31). *Perception: Meaning, Definition, Principles and Factors Affecting in Perception*. Psychology

Discussion. https://www.psychologydiscussion.net/percep tion/perception-meaning-definition-principles-and-factors-affecting-in-perception/634

Shristi, D. (2017, March 11). *6 Major Principles of Perceptual Organisation*. Psychology Discussion. https://www.psychology discussion.net/perception/6-major-principles-of-perceptual-organisation-perception-psychology/2965

SoulStarter, LLC. (n.d.)*Understanding the Subconscious Mind*. Soul Starter. https://www.soulstarter.com/pages/learn-about-the-subconscious-mind

Thinking Traps: How to Let Go of Negative Thoughts. (2019, November 8). The Chelsea Psychology Clinic. https://www.thechelseapsychologyclinic.com/mood-management/thinking-traps/

Ultimate goal setting process: 7 steps to creating better goals. (2018, February 6) Lucid Content Team. https://www.lucidchart.com/blog/the-ultimate-goal-setting-process-in-7-steps

What does Deepak Chopra's daily routine look like? (2019, September 27). The Optimist Daily. https://www.optimistdaily.com/2019/09/what-does-deepak-chopras-daily-routine-look-like/

Winfrey, O. (2011, August). *What Oprah Knows for Sure About Trusting Her Intuition*. Oprah.com. https://www.oprah.com/spirit/oprah-on-trusting-her-intuition-oprahs-advice-on-trust ing-your-gut

IMAGE REFERENCES

Akyurt, E. (2017). *Coffee-pen-notebook-open-notebook* [Image]. Pixabay. https://pixabay.com/photos/coffee-pen-notebook-open-notebook-2306471/

Altmann, G. (2017). *Ladder-beyond-clouds-heaven* [Image]. Pixabay. https://pixabay.com/photos/ladder-beyond-clouds-heaven-2748333/

Altmann, G. (2018). *Never-stop-learning* [Image]. Pixabay. https://pixabay.com/photos/never-stop-learning-3653430/

Altmann, G. (2019). *Stairs-stages-feet-legs-success* [Image]. Pixabay. https://pixabay.com/photos/stairs-stages-feet-legs-success-4574579/

Fotorech. (2017). *Woman-sky-sunlight-arms-open-arms* [Image]. Pixabay. https://pixabay.com/photos/woman-sky-sunlight-arms-open-arms-2667455/

Hain, J. (2014). *Mind-brain-mindset-perception* [Image]. Pixabay. https://pixabay.com/illustrations/mind-brain-mindset-perception-544404/

Hernandez, J. (2022). *Maslow Pyramid.* Canva. https://www.canva.com/design/DAFSWTVzLGY/UouAEWvrPk34Wll0xQ7qIg/view?utm_content=DAFSWTVzLGY&utm_campaign=designshare&utm_medium=link&utm_source=publishsharelink

Kalhh. (2016). *Block-lamp-get-dream-goal-path* [Image]. Pixabay. https://pixabay.com/illustrations/block-lamp-get-dream-goal-path-1512119/

Possible-impossible-opportunity [Image]. (2015). Pixabay. https://pixabay.com/illustrations/possible-impossible-opportunity-953169/

Ramdlon, F. (2015). *Creative-be-creative-write-bulb* [Image]. Pixabay. https://pixabay.com/photos/creative-be-creative-write-bulb-725811/

Studio, L. (2015). *Woman-stretch-fitness-outdoor* [Image]. Pixabay. https://pixabay.com/photos/woman-stretch-fitness-outdoor-4127336/